HEARTBREAK AND HOPE

A Homecoming Story

of the

Houghton Six

Houghton University

with Jack Connell

wesleyan
PUBLISHING HOUSE
wphstore.com
Fishers, IN

Library of Congress Cataloging-in-Publication Data

Names: Houghton University, author. | Connell, Jack, author.
Title: Heartbreak and hope: a homecoming story of the Houghton six /
   Houghton University with Jack Connell.
Description: Fishers, Indiana: Wesleyan Publishing House, [2024] |
   Includes bibliographical references. | Summary: "At the time of their
   matriculation to Houghton, for nearly a century already, the college had
   positively and profoundly impacted the living and learning of
   generations of students. Like Houghton students today, I imagine it was
   different combinations of family history, location, athletics, and the
   promise of a transformational Christian education that drew Mark, Beth,
   Alan, Joy, Albert, and Cyndy to Houghton in 1978. Each student
   individually became a leader and impacted the college and student body
   in indelible ways. Together, their deaths would impact Houghton forever.
   Their names and memories are forever enshrined in Houghton's history,
   and in the hearts and minds of Highlanders, past and present"-- Provided
   by publisher.
Identifiers: LCCN 2024031913 (print) | LCCN 2024031914 (ebook) | ISBN
   9781632576620 (paperback) | ISBN 9781632576637 (ebook)
Subjects: LCSH: Houghton University--History--20th century. | College
   students--New York (State)--Houghton--Social conditions. | Traffic
   accidents--New York (State)--Houghton--History--20th century. |
   Christian universities and colleges--New York
   (State)--Houghton--History--20th century.
Classification: LCC LD2281.H732 H68 2024 (print) | LCC LD2281.H732
   (ebook) | DDC 378.747/84--dc23/eng/20240821
LC record available at https://lccn.loc.gov/2024031913
LC ebook record available at https://lccn.loc.gov/2024031914

For

Mark Bertram Anderson

May 4, 1960—October 2, 1981

Beth Renee Andes

February 12, 1960—October 2, 1981

Alan Robert Bushart

July 15, 1960—October 2, 1981

Joy Suzanne Ellis

October 8, 1960—October 2, 1981

Albert Lester Rapp Jr.

April 10, 1960—October 2, 1981

Cynthia Rae Rudes

September 9, 1960—October 2, 1981

And for their families.

And all who knew and loved them.

Those who hope in the Lord will renew their strength.

They will soar on wings like eagles;

they will run and not grow weary,

they will walk and not be faint.

(Isaiah 40:31)

CONTENTS

FOREWORD

Jesus wept.
John 11:35

With over 140 years of history, Houghton's lengthy story is deep and wide. But any telling of this story is incomplete without a recounting and consideration of The Six and the tragedy of October 2, 1981.

At the time of their matriculation to Houghton, for nearly a century already, the college had positively and profoundly impacted the living and learning of generations of students. Like Houghton students today, I imagine it was different combinations of family history, location, athletics, and the promise of a transformational Christian education that drew Mark, Beth, Alan, Joy, Albert, and Cindy to Houghton in 1978. Each student individually became a leader and impacted the college and student body in indelible ways. Together, their deaths would impact Houghton forever. Their names and memories are forever enshrined in Houghton's history, and in the hearts and minds of Highlanders, past and present.

With this work of love, Dr. Jack Connell captures and shares the stories of the six young, beautiful lives lost on that fateful morning in 1981. He further shares the story of a college community, families, and loved ones wracked with grief and pain, who question, seek understanding and healing, and hold fast to hope and their Christian faith.

In October 1981, in its humanity, Houghton wept with the Anderson, Andes, Bushart, Ellis, Rapp, and Rudes families. Even today, Houghton weeps, but not as those without hope (see 1 Thess. 4:13). My prayer is that this volume honors the lives and contributions of The Six, is helpful in bringing further healing to their families and loved ones, brings new light to a tragic time in Houghton's history, and through it all, glorifies God.

WAYNE D. LEWIS JR., PHD
PRESIDENT

HOUGHTON'S 9/11

Each generation shares rare moments that nearly everyone can describe precisely where they were, who they were with, and what they were doing when they heard the news. Events that are seared into our collective memories. Moments when time seemed to stand still. Moments that define a generation.

For my grandparents' generation, World War II provided several of these heart-stopping moments in rapid succession: Pearl Harbor on December 7, 1941, D-Day on June 6, 1944, and V-E Day on May 8, 1945.

For my parents' generation, there were the assassinations of the tumultuous 1960s: President John F. Kennedy on November 23, 1963, Dr. Martin Luther King Jr. on April 4, 1968, and Senator Robert F. Kennedy on June 6, 1968, as well as Neil Armstrong's "giant leap for mankind" on July 21, 1969.

For my generation, the explosion of the space shuttle *Challenger* on January 28, 1986, and the death of Princess Diana on August 31, 1996, are branded into our hearts.

For my children's generation, only two numbers are needed—9/11.

For most people, October 2, 1981, is not that kind of momentous date. That day's *New York Times* headline described President Ronald Reagan's relationship with Saudi Arabia—important, sure, but hardly generation defining. Perhaps for some, this was a landmark birthday or anniversary or some other occasion of personal significance. But for most, it is another day lost to the blurring of memory and the fog of history. Utterly unremarkable. Wholly forgettable. Unless, that is, you are a member of the Anderson, Andes, Bushart, Ellis, Rapp, or Rudes families. Unless you or a loved one were on the campus of Houghton College, a small Christian college in rural western New York State, that fateful day. For those of us who were, October 2, 1981, is likely as memorable and profound and tragic a day as any we've experienced. We can tell you where we were, who we were with, and what we were doing when we heard the news. The news of the frightful car accident. The news of The Six who had been lost. The news that took our breath away.

My memories from that day are clear and agonizing. After what must have been an unusually grueling week, I took a Friday afternoon nap in the off-campus house I shared with six other Houghton students. When I woke up around dinner time, I was the only one still in the house; the others had already walked down the hill to campus for dinner or left campus for their Friday evening plans. I walked alone to dinner, taking a trail through the woods and turning left on Park Drive near campus. Walking along the road by Paine Science Center, a classmate walked toward me. I greeted her cheerfully: "Hi Kirsten!"

"You haven't heard yet, have you?" she responded.

"Heard what?"

Even now, I can picture her distressed face as she told me that six students had been killed in a car accident. She said she wasn't sure of all their names, but she thought they were all members of the homecoming court.

In disbelief, I walked hurriedly across the grassy quad, taking the most direct line to the Reinhold Campus Center. I climbed a handful of steps and entered the campus center's lounge—the spacious "living room" of the campus, with floor-to-ceiling windows that looked back over the quad and multiple sofas and comfortable chairs grouped conveniently for conversation with friends. On a Friday evening at dinnertime, the lounge was normally alive with laughter and banter, as students talked excitedly about their weekend plans or gathered with friends before walking up the wide wooden stairway to the second-floor dining hall. As I entered the lounge, though, all I heard was an uneasy silence, broken only by muffled whispers and occasional sobs. Groups of students were huddled together around the large room—some hugging, some praying, many dabbing at the tears in their eyes. I don't remember who told me, but there I first heard the full story: that the six senior members of the homecoming court—Beth and Mark, Cindy and Al, Joy and Bert—had all been killed in a car accident near Buffalo.

People sometimes describe Houghton (and small colleges in general) as a "bubble"—a cocoon-like atmosphere where students are carefully protected from the evils and troubles of the "real" world. On October 2, 1981, any Houghton bubble was pierced—obliterated—with grief and shock and loss. I knew all six students, although as a junior I was one year behind them and not best friends with any. Joy and Bert were business majors, as was I, so we had many classes together. I knew Mark through our shared involvement in student government and was acquainted with Beth through him. I knew Al and Cindy through friends who were close to the members of the soccer and volleyball teams. Houghton is a small college, and like the 1980s TV show *Cheers*, it's a place where virtually "everybody knows your name." And these six were prominent and popular leaders on campus; everybody knew their names.

This book is the story of their lives, deaths, and legacies. It is the story of friends and families and a community. It is the story of love and loss, strength and weakness, faith and doubt. It is a story that is told to preserve the memories of The Six with the hope that revisiting these events and sharing how people responded to them will provide grace and comfort for the losses that inevitably enter all of our lives.

I have believed for at least twenty years now that someone should write this story. I started the project nearly ten years ago, but deferred to someone else who was also interested in taking it on. Unfortunately, that person was ultimately unable to do so. Then, in the summer of 2023, at our forty-year reunion, a group of Houghton classmates and I gathered around a campus firepit and stayed up late telling stories and laughing about our college days. The eagles sculpture honoring The Six was only a few steps away and loomed over our reminiscing. When the conversation inevitably turned to the accident, the laughter quickly faded, and long silences punctuated the conversation. As I looked around the circle at the solemn faces of my friends, staring pensively into the flames, I quietly determined to start again. Others are certainly more qualified to tell this story, but I have done my best to give you a faithful and meaningful account of the students, what transpired, and how the impact of their lives and deaths continues to reverberate in the lives of so many.

Two explanatory notes are in order. First, I refer to people and places as they were known at the time they appear in the story. For example, the institution is referred to as Houghton College when writing about 1981 and Houghton University when writing about the present. Students are referenced with the names they used as students; name changes due to marriage are used when referring to them later in life and in the citations at the end of the book. Second, while I make abundant use of the available primary sources, I am also dependent upon what people remember of events that happened more than forty years ago. Human memory can be a tricky thing, especially when so much time has elapsed. Consequently, I have attempted to include only those memories about which people are confident or those that can be corroborated by another person or primary source. I have excluded recollections that were expressed to me with vagueness or uncertainty—or noted them as such.

—Jack Connell

ACKNOWLEDGMENTS

I have often referred to this book as a labor of love, but the love invested has not been merely my own. As a solo act, this book would have remained only an idea. I am profoundly indebted to the dozens of people who made this labor of love their own and have offered their support, encouragement, and input.

It was my privilege to speak with several family members of The Six who were lost. A person's grief is a sacred, tender space and I am so grateful for their willingness to open that space to me. Tears often flowed freely during these conversations. Thank you to Keith Anderson and Terry Anderson, brothers of Mark Anderson; Mindy Andes, sister of Beth Andes; Warren Bushart and Kevin Bushart, brothers of Alan Bushart; Barbara Isaman Bushart, sister-in-law of Alan Bushart; and Debbie Rudes Haas, sister of Cindy Rudes.

The three most recent presidents of Houghton College/University all offered their kind support to this project. Dr. Daniel Chamberlain, president at the time of the accident and "my" president, generously shared his remembrances with me just a few months before his passing. I will cherish my memories of that final conversation with him. Dr. Shirley Mullen supported this project in its infancy, gave me the opportunity to speak about the accident at the scarf ceremony when I served in her administration, and provided words of reflection that appear in the final chapter. Dr. Wayne Lewis,

Houghton's current president, took a leap of faith on me by endorsing the project and kindly agreed to write the foreword.

Thank you to the Houghton alumni who were students at the college or the academy in the early 1980s and graciously shared their memories of The Six, the accident, and the ways in which their lives were impacted by all that happened: Bill Allen, Cindy Prentice Austin, Kirsten Dyal Barton, Erma Mekeel Boswell, Mary Beth Fuller Bowling, Jon Bradley, Glenn Burlingame, Janet Carlson Tennies, Betsy Lundell Carosa, Mark Christopher, Kevin Danielson, Brian Davidson, Chris Schmitt Davidson, Dexter Davis, Mercy Zecher Dawson, Scott Dawson, Cindy Brenner Dey, Graham Drake, Steve Dunbar, Marlene Gifford, Kristina Hansen, Karyn Hecht, Allen Hemayakian, Jon Horton, Rob Jacobsen, Steve Jacobsen, Jeff Jordan, Jan Merz Kennedy, Jeff LaDine, Judy Tennant Mahoney, Gregg Makin, Martha Manikas-Foster, Troy Martin, Andrew Mullen, James Mullen, Janet Franz Nelson, Tim Nichols, Becca Thorn Oehrig, Mark Ohl, Doug Roorbach, Rob Ruth, Brian Segool, Tedd Smith, Ed Taylor, Tammy Willis, Meg Martino Wright, and Betty Bowser Young. It was truly a delight to reconnect with so many former schoolmates and friends.

Thank you to those who served as members of the faculty, staff, or administration at Houghton in the 1980s and shared their insights and encouragement with me: Mark Abbott, Bud Bence, Kathie Brenneman, Doug Burke, Robert Danner, Bill Doezema, Connie Finney, David Frazier, Tanya Shire Hildebrandt, Richard "Jake" Jacobsen, Tom Kettlekamp, Harold Kingdon, Dean Liddick, Wayne MacBeth, Charles Massey, Larry Mullen, Ray Parlett, Dick Pocock, Sandy Roederer, Brian Sayers, Fred Shannon, Phil Stockin, Mike Walters, and Paul Young. I hold all of you in high regard.

Several current members of the staff and faculty of Houghton University lent their assistance. Greg Bish, chief of staff, and Dale Wright, vice president of finance, were my liaisons to Houghton throughout the process of research and writing and met with me regularly to keep me out of trouble and on budget. Their assistance with the many on-campus logistics was invaluable. Ted Murphy, Professor of Art at Houghton since 1986 and my former neighbor, kindly allowed us to use his beautiful artwork on the cover: Yellow Leaf (2020). Phyllis Gaerte, director of alumni relations, assisted with all communication with alumni and friends of the college. David Stevick, director of the library, and Taylor Stuck, archivist, patiently assisted in my efforts to track down all manner of documents and recordings. Matt Webb, director of athletics, and Jason Mucher, director of sports information, helped me gather information related to the three who were student athletes and invited me to a beautiful event held in their memory. John Oden, director of advancement services, chased down a variety of data points for me. Dan Noyes, regional director of development, provided information about the genesis of the scarf ceremony. Kevin Kettinger, registrar, provided access to college catalogs from the 1980s. Karl Sisson, vice president of advancement, provided information about endowments given in memory of The Six. And Dean Liddick, retired director of public information, was relentless in his pursuit of photos and articles that proved immensely helpful in this effort.

A classmate of The Six wrote an anonymous essay about the accident called "Joy Forever" and left it in the alumni office during homecoming weekend 2021. The alumni office and I have done our best to uncover the identity of the author, but so far without success. I am grateful to the author for his fine work and hope he will one day come forward so that we can give appropriate attribution.

Mark Chamberlain, son of Dr. and Mrs. Dan Chamberlain, provided me with some of Dr. Chamberlain's correspondence from the time of the accident and a wonderful biography of his parents that he recently wrote. Nathan Danner researched information available through the Houghton Wesleyan Church.

Several people outside the Houghton family have kindly offered their assistance as well. Ron Becker, retired chief of the Wales Center Volunteer Fire Company, was one of the first to arrive at the accident scene and provided his first-hand account. Chief Held and Sergeant Parici of the Erie County Sheriff's Office secured for me the police report of the accident. Robert Lowell Goller, Aurora town historian, and Patricia Spahn, Town of Wales historian, provided me with helpful local resources and connections. Chris Carosa, an author and historian, very generously shared with me his own research about the accident. I'm grateful as well to the many journalists who wrote about the accident in the days immediately afterward; their contemporaneous accounts enriched the narrative immeasurably.

I am deeply grateful for the wonderful partnership of colleagues and friends at Wesleyan Publishing House. Susan LeBaron was enthusiastic in her support of the project and masterful in her management of the many details. She kept us all on track and helped us meet an ambitious timeline. Kevin Scott's editorial insights strengthened and clarified my writing and unquestionably made this a better book. Lyn Rayn's excellent design work is evident on the cover and throughout the book.

My entire family has been wonderfully supportive of me in this endeavor. I'm grateful to my daughter Rebekah, whose skills as an archivist were indispensable as I started my research and who also took the time to read an early draft and provide helpful feedback. My son David provided some IT wizardry that allowed me to retrieve from an old computer some preliminary research I had done several years ago; without that critical assistance, this project likely would not have gotten off the ground. I believe my sons Jonathan and Michael have promised to read it. Finally, I could never have begun or sustained this project without the loving support, patience, and encouragement of my wife, Wendy. The irony is not lost on me that she was Houghton's homecoming queen in the fall of 1985, just four years after the accident, and so I am beyond grateful for her life, love, and willingness to support our household while I took a year "off" to write this book. She will be happy to know that I can now get back to having a real job.

These acknowledgments are accompanied by the nagging sense that I have probably omitted someone who made vital contributions. Please accept my apologies and be assured that my failure to name you stems only from a memory lapse or an error in record keeping, not from any lack of appreciation.

Despite the generous contributions of so many, I take sole responsibility for any errors that may be present in the account that follows. On behalf of everyone who shared my love for this project, I give this story to you with gratitude to God and thankfulness for the privilege I had of knowing Mark, Beth, Al, Joy, Bert, and Cindy. I hope to have done justice to their memory and to be able to see them again one day.

THE SIX

HOMECOMING COURT

It was not a beauty pageant that determined who would be Houghton's homecoming queen in the autumn of years gone by. When the members of the senior class gathered in September to elect three nominees from among their classmates, it was not an effort to identify who was prettiest. Rather, it was a way to acknowledge those who were most deeply loved and admired. Although the young women selected might in fact be outwardly attractive, appearance was at most an ancillary consideration. The nominees for homecoming queen were selected each fall because of the character qualities they exhibited during their years at Houghton—engagement, kindness, servant-leadership, and Christian commitment. The beauty that was prized was beauty of spirit. When the members of the class of 1982 selected Beth Andes, Joy Ellis, and Cindy Rudes as their nominees, they were holding these three young women up as models of devotion and goodness—exemplars of the values of the Houghton community and classmates who the seniors would be proud to have representing them.

Each of the three candidates for homecoming queen invited an escort who would accompany her for the festivities. Beth Andes and Cindy Rudes each selected their long-term boyfriends: Mark Anderson and Alan Bushart, respectively. Joy

Ellis' boyfriend attended another college, so she selected as her escort a friend for whom she had great respect and admiration—Bert Rapp. Together, the six students comprised the senior members of the homecoming court. They would ride on the senior class float during the homecoming parade, represent the class at a variety of homecoming functions, and, in what was considered a highlight of homecoming weekend, one of the three young women would be named homecoming queen at the coronation ceremony.

The Six weren't perfect. They were barely out of their teenage years and had flaws, foibles, and failings just like the rest of us. But they were, as President Chamberlain said at the time, "six of the school's most popular, most dedicated, most energetic leaders. Six seniors who were so well-equipped to face life."[1] The purpose of this chapter is not to canonize them, but simply to provide brief profiles of each so that we can remember them. And to acknowledge the gifts and graces that were given to them by God, lovingly nurtured by their families, and then shared with the campus community and the world for an all-too-brief time period.

— MARK ANDERSON —

The third of four brothers, Mark Anderson was born in the kitchen of the family home in Lancaster, Pennsylvania, on May 4, 1960.[2] Although the *Star Wars* pun of "May the Fourth be with you" did not exist until after his death, Mark's family is convinced he would have loved it. The Andersons moved to upstate New York when Mark was in elementary school and to Danielson, Connecticut, a small town near the Rhode Island border, when he was in junior high. Mark's father, Bert, was a blue-collar worker who taught himself mechanics and rose through the ranks at International Paper, ultimately becoming a plant and regional manager. His mother, Doris (Blakney) Anderson, was a real estate agent who became one of the top realtors in northeastern Connecticut. Neither had the opportunity to attend college, so it was important to them that each of their four sons—Keith, Terry, Mark, and Kevin—receive an education. Devout Christians, the family attended a large, conservative church, whose leadership began to exhibit some autocratic, cult-like characteristics. The Anderson family ultimately made the difficult decision to leave the church and encouraged their sons to be willing always to think for themselves and ask hard questions of those in authority.

Mark was a baseball enthusiast, with an extensive collection of autographed cards and a passion for playing the Strat-o-matic baseball board game. He was not a gifted athlete, but he made up for his modest skills with effort and tenacity. After getting cut from the high school basketball team, he practiced incessantly in the family driveway and made the team the following year. Always interested in government and politics, he participated in the civics program Boys State while in high school. He had a keen mind and a sharp wit, but also a gracious spirit. Mark's older brothers describe him as the sibling who was able to ease the inevitable tensions that arose among the four boys, typically with a well-timed humorous quip or a gentle word of encouragement. One brother said Mark was "the mortar between the bricks"; another referred to him as "the oil in the engine."[3] Mark was especially close with his mother, who welcomed his encouragement and support. He graduated with honors from Killingly High School in 1978 and, like his older brothers before him, enrolled at Houghton College.

At Houghton, Mark began preparing for a career in law as a history major in the pre-law program; he had minors in speech, sociology, political science, and philosophy.[4] Mark viewed the legal profession as an opportunity to right some of the wrongs he saw in the world. He applied his sharp intellect to his studies and to a variety of co-curricular activities that reflected his career plans. Mark was heavily involved in Student Senate and served on the Student Development Council, the Campus Activities Board, and the Judicial Committee.[5] Although he was not elected Student Senate president his senior year, the person who edged Mark for the office relied heavily on his wisdom. In a letter to Mark's parents, in which she posthumously awarded Mark the Senate's Presidential Excellence Award, Susan Facer wrote: "Beginning with his freshman year, Mark used his keen analytical abilities to serve the Houghton Community through the Student Senate. Mark could be counted on to interject crucial considerations into any discussion on the Senate floor. . . . Mark was especially helpful to me as I fulfilled my responsibilities as president. He would often stop in my office to sit and chat, and I would take these opportunities to seek out his opinion on matters under consideration."[6] Beyond his involvement in Student Senate, Mark was a member of the debate club, the history honors society, and the MacMillan's Company (a club that facilitated connections between students and alumni); served as a class president; and participated in intramural sports.[7] Additionally, Mark spent the fall semester of his junior year interning at a law firm in Washington, DC.[8] He was honored for his curricular and co-curricular achievements by selection for *Who's Who Among Students in American Colleges and Universities*.[9]

A retired member of the history faculty remembers Mark as "very bright and very funny."[10] Almost without fail, those two qualities are mentioned prominently by those who knew Mark. He had "a great mind," was "super-smart," and "had a powerful, often overwhelming intellect."[11] A student who served with Mark in the Student Senate remembers feeling somewhat intimidated by Mark because he was "such an intellectual" and "always had everything thought out."[12] But Mark didn't take himself or others too seriously and could always be counted on to provide a laugh. "Every meal with Mark was punctuated with laughter."[13] When attending a formal Houghton banquet, he brought levity (and some criticism) by choosing to wear sneakers with his suit.[14] With a small group of friends, he climbed to the off-limits balcony of the landmark belltower on campus and shouted greetings to passersby.[15] I (Jack) remember a Student Senate meeting in which a class senator was obviously and rather pompously trying to impress his peers by using the word *pontificate* in his argument. Mark spoke next and said: "Madam Chair, I have just one question. What does *pontificate* mean?" His quip brought down the house because we all knew that Mark needed no definition and was instead poking fun at his peer.[16]

Mark had a questioning mind. He was committed to a spirit of critical inquiry that challenged assumptions, evaluated arguments, and wouldn't countenance the blind acceptance of the status quo. He had a "healthy skepti-cism" about institutions and ideas; he tended to think "God is great; preachers ain't."[17] In an editorial that appeared in the student newspaper a couple weeks before he died, Mark wrote: "As a part of our Christian desire to better under-stand God and his world, we must be receptive to viewpoints that do not coincide with our own (possibly ill-advised) opinions. As we allow our views to clash with others, an evaluating process occurs. Our godly reason permits us, with the unconscious assistance of the Holy Spirit's illuminating power, to consider how legitimate our beliefs really are."[18] Mark embodied this intellec-tual honesty and courage by his willingness to ask hard questions of faculty members, chapel speakers, peers, and himself. He once gave a speech in chapel in which he presented a thoughtful critique of "the pledge"—Houghton's behavioral expectations for students.[19] A friend commented: "Mark was a won-derfully refreshing Houghtonite. I loved his willingness to pop the bubble and look at things from outside the official perspective."[20]

Mark was "extremely serious about Christianity," and his propensity to ask questions extended into matters of Christian faith and practice.[21] Here the influence of his parents and his family's straitjacketed experience in their authoritarian former church were undoubtedly profound. Twenty-five years after his death, Mark's parents reflected on his faith: "Mark had a profound, ever-deepening commitment to his faith that was refined and burnished among like believers at Houghton. He had an intellectual curiosity and integ-rity that spurred him to try to cut through the shallow platitudes and accepted dogma to find the truth. Houghton provided an environment of shared belief that enabled him to learn, to question, and to challenge his beliefs, leading him to an ever-deepening commitment to Christ."[22] Mark's journal reflects his commitment to thinking carefully about Christian faith, with lengthy entries on such topics as apologetics, ethics, and love. Two brief portions from his entry on May 24, 1981, seem to capture Mark's ethos: "We should spend more time thinking about Christianity and less time feeling Christianity" and "We choose to believe what we want to believe, often regardless of the veracity of the claim."[23]

Mark's family was the object of his great devotion and affection. A picture of "the four boys" was prominent in his room on campus, and he referred to it as he told stories to friends about his beloved brothers.[24] He often bragged about his father's climb to a management position without a college degree and always spoke of his mother with tenderness.[25] When Mark went home to Connecticut on weekends, his mother was intensely interested in the college life she had never experienced. "Sit right here next to me and tell me all about it," she'd say.[26] One of his brothers reflects: "We were very close as brothers and as a family. We would always find joy in the other's successes, and we were always concerned for one another when there were challenges."[27]

Mark's standard summer job involved work in his father's plant, but consistent with his adventurous spirit, he spent his final summer driving taxi in Ketchikan, Alaska, with three Houghton friends. He typically drove the 7 p.m. to 7 a.m. shift and encountered a fascinating array of denizens of the night. "Only once," his brother quipped, "did someone put a knife to his throat."[28]

Mark was planning on law school after graduation, with the Cornell University law school at the top of his list.[29] He aspired to contribute to society in meaningful ways, to make the world a little better. "He would have had a significant career. He was on the cusp of so much. He would have made a mark," commented a friend who was with him in Alaska.[30] Sadly, another sentence from Mark's journal entry on May 24, 1981, was eerily prescient: "Life is not full of happy endings."[31]

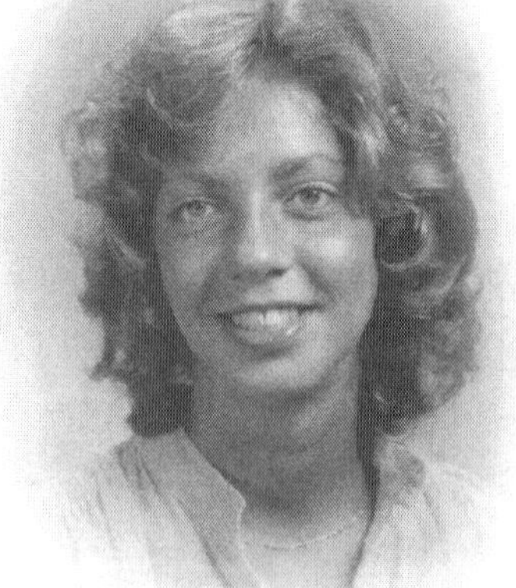

— BETH ANDES —

The home of Gerald and Betty Jane (Kriebel) Andes was filled with music.[32] Jerry was well-known in Pottstown, Pennsylvania, as the owner of a plumbing business. Betty Jane was a devoted homemaker. But it was their love of music that animated their lives. Neither had professional training, but both were skilled vocalists and instrumentalists who were singularly focused on using their talents to serve the Lord. Jerry led worship in church, Betty Jane sang in a women's trio, and together they were a popular vocal duet that performed at numerous churches in the greater Philadelphia area. Their three daughters—Mindy, Patty, and Beth—cut their teeth in a home that prized music as a gift from God and viewed it as a way to glorify God and lead others in worship. Mr. and Mrs. Andes were "amazing role models" of Christian faith, service, and commitment.[33]

The two eldest sisters, Mindy and Patty, were born about a year and a half apart. Beth arrived five years later, on February 12, 1960. Beth's older sisters loved their baby sister and frequently vied for her attention. Once the two older girls were each tugging on one of Beth's arms, trying to pull Beth away from the other. When one of Beth's arms popped out of joint from the tug-of-war, Mindy and Patty quickly deescalated their arguments over their precious little sister. As the youngest, Beth was the apple of her father's eye. They had a relationship that was "always so endearing and special."[34] Like her sisters, Beth began learning piano at an early age. Her musical talent was evident from the start, and before long she also began playing the flute. Because of her parents' extensive involvement in musical ministry, Beth had abundant opportunities to develop and utilize her own gifts—playing hymns and gospel songs in their local church and at a nearby Lancaster mission, where the Andes family provided music and spoke on a monthly basis.

Beth was quiet but also had a presence and charisma that made her influential among her peers. When she entered Pottsgrove High School, the prevailing fashion sense was typical 1970s sloppy—jeans and T-shirts. Beth had learned from her mother, a skilled seamstress, how to sew her own clothes, and she enjoyed going to school in beautiful, handcrafted dresses. Beth's habit of dressing more formally influenced the fashion choices of her peers so noticeably that the principal wrote a letter to Mr. and Mrs. Andes expressing his appreciation for how they raised Beth and for her positive impact on the school. During high school, Beth's faith was nurtured at the Pottstown Youth Center. A Saturday night youth ministry, it attracted many hundreds of teens from the entire region with well-known Christian speakers, movies, music (which her parents helped lead), and fun. As her faith grew, Beth became a dynamic witness for Christ in her high school: "She had no qualms about sharing her faith and what made her tick."[35] Beth excelled musically and came to be regarded as the most gifted musician in her family and one of the premiere musicians in her high school. She graduated from Pottsgrove High School in 1978, with dreams of one day playing the flute professionally in a symphony orchestra.

Beth came to Houghton College in the fall of 1978 as an applied flute major. She was a well-rounded student who was diligent in all her classes, but she gave herself to her studies in music with particular dedication. She met and exceeded the rigorous practice expectations for a flute major and performed with excellence in the symphony orchestra, wind ensemble, and concert band. Every Saturday during the school year, Beth drove with a classmate to Rochester, New York, to take additional private lessons with a flautist who performed with the Rochester Philharmonic Orchestra.[36] As accomplished as she was on the flute, Beth's musical interests and talents extended beyond that one instrument; she was also a talented pianist and was learning to play the alto saxophone. Like her mother and father, she had a beautiful singing voice and sang with the chapel choir. She also enjoyed composing Christian songs and expressed to friends her hope of devoting more time to composition in the future. Beth wanted everything that she did with music to be honoring to God.[37]

Studies in the music department were so demanding that music majors frequently had time for little else; conventional wisdom around campus was that music majors "lived in the music building." Not so with Beth. Likely inspired by her parents' monthly trips to the mission in Lancaster, Beth was actively involved in Allegany County Outreach—a ministry of the college to area children who lived in poverty. Beth served on the cabinet of that organization and selflessly participated in numerous parties and outreach activities that were developed to enrich the lives of the children. Beth also made time to serve on the Cultural Affairs Council, the Music Education Club, and the Brookside Dorm Council, and played intramural volleyball.[38]

Just as Beth learned from her parents to love music and serve others, she also learned from them the importance of living in vital union with Jesus Christ. Shortly after learning of Beth's death, Mr. Andes commented: "She had a personal relationship with the Lord. That was her life."[39] Beth viewed her daily quiet time with God as the most important part of her day.[40] She had developed a plan for memorizing and meditating on Scripture verses and posted note cards with those verses around her dorm room and practice room so that she could regularly be reminded to depend upon the Lord.[41] She was "deeply concerned" about the spiritual lives of others, and in spite of her busy schedule, she always had time to listen, extend care, and pray with fellow students and friends.[42] She was "always lovely and gracious."[43] She understood that her sense of worth did not come from the approval of others, but from God alone.[44] The evangelistic heart Beth had in high school continued in her college years, as she prayed for friends who did not share her faith in Christ—including her flute instructor in Rochester.[45]

Beth's closest friend wrote these words of tribute: "She was a beautiful woman, in outward appearance but especially in spirit. Her Christian testimony will forever stand before me as an example. Not an example of one who was perfect, but of one who was striving in every way to become what the Lord wanted her to be. Supreme in all her decisions was her desire to follow the Lord's will."[46] The prayer of St. Francis of Assisi, which Beth wanted sung at her senior flute recital and at her wedding, reflected her heart's desire:

> Lord, make me an instrument of thy peace. Where there is hatred, let me sow love. Where there is injury, pardon. Where there is doubt, faith. Where there is despair, hope. Where there is darkness, light. Where there is sadness, joy. O Divine Master, grant that I may not so much seek to be consoled as to console. To be understood, as to understand. To be loved, as to love. For it is in giving that we receive. It is in pardoning that we are pardoned. It is in dying that we are born to eternal life.[47]

Beth's aspirations for life after Houghton included pursuing a graduate degree in flute and then a career as a flautist in a symphony orchestra. Her family believed that "the Lord had some really big plans for her in the music field."[48] Speaking in a church service shortly before she died, Beth expressed another hope she had for her future: "I can't wait to get to heaven, so I can see Jesus."[49]

— ALAN BUSHART —

Stanley and Isabelle Bushart raised their seven children in Marion, New York, a small community twenty miles east of Rochester.[50] Stanley worked for the Penn Central Railroad and then started his own furnace repair business. Isabelle was a special education teacher, who often brought students home for the weekend to give their families a respite. The Bushart home was full and busy, and Alan, the sixth child of the seven, was born on July 15, 1960. An intense, high-energy boy, he was, as his mom would say, "a little dickens."[51] His brother Kevin remembers an occasion when Mr. Bushart thought Alan deserved a spanking and Alan took off running, his father futilely chasing him with a yardstick. The episode ended with the entire family collapsed in laughter.

The Busharts were active in their local church and, in the summer, sent the children to a nearby Christian camp. Alan committed his life to Christ at that camp when he was seven or eight years old and, while "he didn't turn into an angel," Alan took his Christian faith very seriously.[52] When family members walked by his bedroom in the morning before school, they would see Alan reading his Bible. When he was about ten, on a dare, Alan put stones in the gas tank of a neighbor's tractor. Later, the owner of the tractor showed the family a letter that Alan had written. In a young boy's handwriting, the letter expresses remorse for what he had done, explains his Christian commitment, and offers all his paper route money to pay for the damages. Alan carried a small Bible to school with him and read a few verses and said a prayer before he ate his lunch. While there was a lot of initial teasing by his peers, by the time he was in high school, other students at his table would bow their heads out of respect when Alan prayed.

Alan's parents taught and modeled the value of hard work, and Alan jumped into his high school career with trademark intensity. An excellent athlete, he was a four-year letterman in track, basketball, and soccer. He could run like the wind and, during his senior year, set a school record and was sectional champion in the two-mile run. He sang the lead role in *Oklahoma!* and other school musicals, went to Bavaria as a foreign exchange student, and maintained an A average in his classes. Alan also found time to sing in the church choir, participate in a variety of church outreach ministries, and even do yard work for elderly neighbors. Alan graduated from Marion High School in 1978 and received the Good Citizenship Award from Daughters of the American Revolution and a Youth Cares Award from Gannett Rochester Newspapers.[53]

Alan came to Houghton College in the fall of 1978 as a music major and sang in the college choir (which selected him as chaplain), the chamber singers, and the traveling ministry group, Son Touched. On Son Touched tours, Al would begin each day by going to the back of the bus alone to spend some time reading the Bible and in prayer.[54] A Son Touched member remembers Al as "just a great guy with such a beautiful voice. He was conscientious and responsible, always did whatever needed to be done. He took the time to get to know every member of the team and was so kind to everyone. Alan was a very warm person, a very talented person, but a very humble person."[55]

As one expression of that humility, Alan was uncertain that he had the ability to play college-level soccer. Coach Doug Burke recalled, though, that "with fierce determination to succeed he made the traveling squad that first year."[56] Al became a four-year starter, a leader on the team, and was selected co-captain his senior year. In the 1979 national tournament for Christian colleges, Al was assigned to defend the leading goal scorer in the nation at any level of college soccer. Al kept him from scoring a single goal, and Houghton won the game and would go on to win the national championship.[57] Teammates remember that Al would never argue or show displeasure with a referee's questionable call.[58] Those who competed against Al remember him muscling them off the ball and then saying a quick "sorry, man" before racing off down the field.[59] Spectators marveled at his sideline throw-ins that would be preceded by a full flip so that he could propel the ball all the way across the field.[60] His best friend and co-captain Brian Davidson recalls: "Al wasn't the best player on any of the four teams, but he was a vital piece of all of them. He was a locomotive. You didn't want to play against him. He was big, thick, fast, and all out. . . . He was a both/and player: he played with a lot of intensity and high energy, but always with the aroma of Christ."[61]

Even more than his outstanding musical and athletic abilities, Al's singular devotion to Christ stood out. In the week after his death, his soccer teammates wrote these words:

> He was looked up to as a close friend, a team leader, and an inspiration for us to hustle as hard as he did. But the most important thing to remember Al for was his love of God.[62]
>
> He was a man that loved the Lord with all his heart and would do anything to glorify the name of Jesus.[63]
>
> As he worked hard, he encouraged me to push myself to limits I had never reached. His enthusiasm helped to unify the team. More than all of this was his love of Christ that I could see in his words and actions on and off the field. He was a servant, a true disciple of Christ. His consistency was a testimony I can't forget.[64]

When Al was asked by a friend how he sustained such a strong Christian witness, he answered that he could count on one hand the days that he missed his quiet time of prayer and Scripture reading.[65] His sister-in-law commented: "He was thoroughly a person of faith. There was no insincerity in him at all; no parts of him that were out of bounds to his faith."[66]

Al's love for God spilled over into genuine love for people. One Thanksgiving break, Al was lamenting the lack of good pizza options around Houghton and encouraged his brother Warren to open a pizza shop in town.[67] The Pizza Barn was born and became an immensely popular hang-out for Houghton students in the 1980s. Al was a part-time employee and regular presence there. One warm summer evening, a college staff member brought her ten-year-old daughter down to the Pizza Barn for ice cream. Al greeted them with his tall white chef's hat on and, on the spot, made up and sang with the young girl a silly song about eating ice cream cones.[68] A faculty member's son who grew up in Houghton remembers Al as one of his heroes—one of the very few Houghton students who both played varsity soccer and sang in the college choir. But even more impressive, he said, was the kindness Alan showed to the young kids in town.[69]

A fellow student recalls: "I saw soccer players as the tough guys, macho, always so impressed with themselves. But that isn't at all who Al was. He wasn't some self-impressed athlete. He was lovely and sweet, and there was always a gentleness to him."[70] Alan was quick to apologize whenever he thought he may have inadvertently hurt or offended someone. His brother joked that if he wanted to torture Alan, all he had to do was respond to Alan's requests for forgiveness with, "I'll think about it. I'm not ready quite yet." Alan always wanted to know that he was at peace with everyone.[71] A teammate said that "Al exuded lovingkindness as he moved through the world."[72] After the accident, Coach Burke commented: "I have not lost a soccer player; I have lost a friend."[73]

Alan switched his major from music to communications so that he could have more classes with his beloved Cindy, who was also a communications major. They were seriously contemplating marriage and were planning to serve the Lord as missionaries together.[74] The Rochester, New York, newspaper aptly summarized Al's life: "In his short life, Alan Bushart drew up an impressive list of accomplishments. He was an athlete and a scholar. He loved his God and his family. Everyone seemed to like him."[75]

One autumn evening at the Pizza Barn, an underclassman was discouraged about his academic work and was considering quitting an important dimension of his studies. Al stopped what he was doing, sat down with the student, and spent some time giving him hope and encouraging him to press on. A college administrator was seated at the next table and could not help but overhear portions of what was said. After the younger student had left, the administrator commented to Al: "I did not mean to eavesdrop on your conversation, but I just want you to know that I think the advice and counsel you gave that young man was the best he could have received anywhere. No professional counselor could have been more adequate."[76] So much of what people loved about Al is reflected in that account—selflessness, sensitivity, wisdom, compassion, kindness. That conversation transpired the evening of October 1, 1981—the night before the accident that took his life.

— JOY ELLIS —

Joy Suzanne Ellis was a pastor's kid who endured the frequent relocations that were common in clergy families of that time. The first church her father pastored after graduating from college was a lovely white church in the countryside of Orange, Vermont, and Joy was born in the nearby community of Barre on October 8, 1960. A few months later, the young pastoral family of Rev. Robert Ellis and his wife Carol (Corby), their son Robert, and baby Joy moved to Brockville, Ontario, Canada, to start a new congregation.[77] After a brief ministry in Brockville, the family moved to Geneva, New York, in the Finger Lakes region of western New York, where Rev. Ellis served as the pastor of Geneva Alliance Church and Joy attended North Street Elementary School.[78] The family lived in Geneva from 1961–1971, and during these years, Joy's brother Don was born. The moves continued as Joy's father served churches in Endicott, New York (1971–1974), and Bowie, Maryland (1974–1976), before moving to Watertown, New York, when Joy was fifteen years old.[79] In Watertown, Rev. Ellis became the pastor of Parkside Bible Church, and Carol worked for Sencon Systems.[80]

Joy entered Watertown High School as a junior and completed her final two years of high school there. During her brief time at Watertown High, she played volleyball, served on the yearbook staff and the Girls' Athletic Association, and was inducted into the National Honor Society.[81] Kim Wallace, a friend of Joy's from Watertown High, remembers her first encounter with Joy: "I first saw her when she came into chemistry class. She was quiet, but you could tell there was something really nice about her, like a ray of sunshine." Kim continued: "Joy was very well named. She brought a piece of joy and a sense of peace to anyone she came into contact with. I can't put it into words . . . she was easy to love and had a lot of love to share with people."[82] The high school principal, Glenn Feistal, remembered Joy as "a very religious girl, a good student and a good citizen."[83] Joy likely would have been active in the small church her father pastored, and a member of that church said of Joy: "She was very sweet, a peach."[84] Joy worked part-time as an assistant with the Watertown Recreation Department and at McDonalds.[85] And for at least one summer, she served as a camp counselor at Delta Lake Bible Camp in Rome, New York, where a girl in her cabin, who would later follow Joy to Houghton College, remembers: "Joy was my counselor-in-training. I was feeling pretty unlovable and lost at that time in my life. Joy struck me with her love for the Lord and her caring way of dealing with me."[86]

Joy came to Houghton in the fall of 1978 and began a double major in physical education and business administration. Her career goal was to become a physical education teacher and coach.[87] For her first three years at Houghton, she played on the women's volleyball team. Joy's coach remembers her as a solid player who wasn't caught up in her own performance, but was more focused on working hard, enjoying the team, and cheering on her teammates.[88] For a time, she served as team chaplain, sharing Scripture readings and poems with her teammates.[89] Joy shared her love for the game and her playing skills with the high school girls at Houghton Academy, where she served as volleyball coach.[90] The diminutive Joy also enjoyed going into tiny, ancient Bedford gymnasium and repeatedly "setting" the ball for the six-foot-six top-scorer on the men's basketball team so that he could practice his spiking.[91] In spite of how much she loved volleyball, Joy decided to forgo her senior year on the team so she could focus more fully on her studies and enjoy her final year with her friends.[92] Beyond volleyball, Joy jumped into campus life as a member of the Student Senate, the Young Administrators Organization, and the Athletics Association, and by participating in club soccer and helping out at the ski slope.[93]

In all her activities and in the way she conducted her entire life, those who remember Joy agree that she could not have been given a more fitting first name. She loved life and loved people and brought joy wherever she went. She talked a friend into buying a Mickey Mouse kite so they could fly it together on the quad in the center of campus.[94] One night Joy was listening to the rain tapping on the roof and said to her roommate: "Isn't it neat, the rain?"

"Joy, it's been raining for four nights!" her roommate responded.

"But doesn't it sound so nice?" Joy answered.[95]

She "led with a smile, "always saw the good things," and was "always bubbly, always doing something fun."[96] One of her faculty members said "Joy was bright and cheerful. All the time."[97] Another said simply "Joy was just joy."[98]

Joy found joy in the simple gifts of life. She invited a large group of friends home with her for a weekend so they could all go sledding.[99] She loved rainbows and wildflowers and eating raw cookie dough batter late at night. She loved hearts and had some attached to her shoelaces. She loved singing along with Amy Grant records. She loved her stuffed animal Tigger, which she would liken to the Velveteen Rabbit and smother with love so it would become real. Joy got excited about so many different things that a housemate imagined her in heaven, repeatedly saying, "Look, you guys, look! Look at how wonderful it is!"[100]

The gift that Joy loved the most, though, was people. She had a "fierce" love for her family, and the bulletin board in her dorm room was festooned with their pictures—along with an arrow that pointed out her dad.[101] Her two final summers she worked as a counselor at Deer Run Christian Camp in New Hampshire, where she went the extra mile to invest in her campers. When she taught waterskiing, she eschewed the typical method of giving instructions from the dock and instead got right in the water so she could be next to the kids.[102] She always had time for her friends, even to the point of getting distracted from her studies. Late night conversations were frequent. Said one of her housemates: "You could talk with her about anything, about your dumbest thoughts, or about God. She'd always find just the right verse for the problem."[103] A student who transferred into Houghton remembers how Joy welcomed her to campus: "Joy was like my big sister; she put her arm around me as I was getting started at Houghton. Such a beautiful spirit."[104] The Sunday before she died, she sat in church with a lonely high school senior and then invited her to have lunch with her in the college cafeteria.[105] The night before the accident, she mailed her boyfriend Tom a few rainbow stickers to cheer him up and a Houghton T-shirt to help him feel at home when he came to visit her for homecoming.[106]

Joy was diligent in her studies and worked hard to keep herself organized. She kept lists for everything—reminders to complete assignments, pray for friends, go to chapel, write her boyfriend.[107] A housemate remembers how Joy would walk around the campus with her stack of books and her list of things to do with little checkboxes. In an effort to help Joy stay on task, she would ask, "Let me see you how your list is coming along," and Joy would invariably say with a smile, "I haven't gotten enough of them done yet!"[108] A poster in Joy's room announced, "I'm so far behind I think I'm first."[109]

Joy typically began her day with a quiet time of prayer and Scripture reading while she ate her cereal. She once commented to a friend: "I'm not ready for Christ to come back for me yet. I'm not ready to die because I've got much more to do."[110] Always humble, she was surprised when she was selected for the homecoming court and thought there were many more qualified candidates. In considering who she would choose as her escort, her top priority was to select someone who shared her deep Christian faith.[111] Each week, Joy nurtured that faith by participating with a small group of students who met in a campus prayer chapel for worship and prayer. One of the group's favorite songs was called "Family" and was originally performed by Joy's favorite artist, Amy Grant. The song ended with Joy and her friends singing these words: "So come join the family. 'Cause we are a family. And we are all going home. Yes, we are all going home."[112]

— BERT RAPP —

Albert Lester (Bert) Rapp Jr. was born on April 10, 1960, to Albert and Mildred (Wilbergh) Rapp of Harrington Park, New Jersey. Bert grew up in the suburbs of northern New Jersey, just a few miles west of the Hudson River and New York City. His father worked in New York City as an executive with the

Bank of New York. Together, Mr. and Mrs. Rapp raised five children—Bert and his four sisters, Muriel, Marilyn, Miriam, and Meredith. Bert graduated from Northern Valley Regional High School in Old Tappan, New Jersey, in 1978. A gifted musician, Bert received the top music award in his high school and was selected for the All-State Chorus in New Jersey his junior and senior year. His mother commented about Bert: "He was six foot five, and just the handsomest boy. Such a good boy."[113]

Inspired by his father's career in business, Bert came to Houghton to study business administration and accounting. He was a diligent and excellent student. A roommate recalls with a chuckle: "Bert was always studying. If we wanted to do something on a weekend, he'd usually say 'Nah, I can't. I've gotta study.'"[114] I (Jack) sat right next to Bert in business finance class and remember his mastery of the complicated principles and formulas. But alongside Bert's deep commitment to his studies was an impressive level of involvement in a wide variety of extracurricular activities. The activities that Bert listed on his student activity form in the fall of 1981 exceeded the allocated space and spilled into the margins: college choir, chamber singers, men's choir, orchestra (he played bass cello), computer club, disc jockey at the campus radio station, and accounting lab assistant. His leadership gifts were evident, as he served as president of the Young Administrators' Organization, the Student Senate's representative to the Financial Affairs Committee of the college, business manager of the *Houghton Star* newspaper, and dorm council president.[115] Unsurprisingly, his academic strength and campus leadership prompted his selection into *Who's Who Among Students in American Colleges and Universities*.[116]

One might expect someone who is so talented to exude an air of grandiosity. To the contrary, Bert's friends describe him as unfailingly humble, kind, gracious, and supportive. "Bert was the gentle giant—a big guy, but so friendly and nice to everybody.[117] "Bert was just a big sweetheart—friendly, warm, a big teddy bear, a kind soul."[118] "Even though he was a high-profile senior and I was a lowly freshman, Bert was so kind and helpful to me. I appreciated and still remember his willingness to reach out to me in my early days on campus."[119] As much as I was impressed by Bert's intellectual gifts in business finance class, I recall even more his willingness to patiently offer help and encouragement to those of us who weren't on his academic level.[120]

Bert possessed an unusual level of maturity for a twenty-one-year-old. His roommate commented: "Bert always seemed older than he was—more dedicated, wiser. He had more purpose, he was more goal-oriented, more serious about what he was doing than most college kids."[121] Another friend noted: "I would have guessed that Bert was ten years older than the rest of us, in a lovely way, because of his stability and demeanor and wisdom."[122] Bert "wouldn't-do-anything-wrong" friends' efforts to get him to bend a rule or skip an assignment were fruitless.[123] Bert managed his finances with a level of care that allowed him to purchase a car, and he was thoughtful and intentional about career planning.[124] One of his business faculty members said: "There was a unique sense of responsibility that Bert had."[125] A college publication wrote: "To remember Bert Rapp is to remember a mature, responsible Christian gentleman."[126]

Yet Bert was also an upbeat, energetic, fun-loving college student. A roommate remembers their shared (and failed) attempt to use stones to build a dam across Houghton Creek, the small stream that ran near campus. "We were just goofing around, being college kids, and Bert loved it."[127] Bert enjoyed pranking his roommates. Once when a roommate went home for the weekend, Bert completely emptied the roommate's side of the room of all furniture and possessions—even taking down the ceiling tiles. When his roommate returned, Bert was hiding in a room across the hallway, but had left a running tape recorder in the room to capture the reaction. Another roommate returned to the house one winter night to find his entire room—bed, desk, lamps, bookcase—set up outside in the snow. When he went inside, he found Bert sitting at his own desk, studying intently, and managing to keep a perfectly straight face.[128] Bert's favorite pop song was "What a Fool Believes" by the Doobie Brothers, and his six-foot-five frame would happily dance around the room when it came on the radio.[129] He would playfully (and carefully) throw snowballs at friends.[130] And in spite of Bert's scrupulousness about keeping the rules, a group of business majors once managed to get Bert to violate one tenet of "the pledge" and join them on the dance floor at a disco in nearby Olean.[131]

Others describe Bert as "always in a good mood, with an ever-present smile."[132] "He was a very confident, yet not arrogant young man. He was a loyal friend and always had time for you regardless of what he had going on."[133] "He was positive, a go-getter. I don't remember him ever being down or negative."[134] He liked to read. He enjoyed taking walks. He dearly loved his four sisters and enjoyed joking about being the only member of the family who would carry on the family name. Bert was shy about girls, and it took substantial prodding from friends to get him to express his interest to a girl on campus he liked.[135]

Central to Bert's sterling character was his deep commitment to Christ. His roommate remembers Bert as "a very serious Christian . . . a person of deep faith." He read his Bible faithfully. He attended worship services at the Houghton Wesleyan Church regularly—"morning service, evening service, we never missed." He eagerly attended chapel. Even when his roommate would point out that a certain number of absences were allowed each semester and that Bert hadn't missed any, Bert would still insist on going.[136] When a journalist asked Bert's father if his son was religious, his father replied: "I'm going to shock you and say no. People confuse religion with knowing the Lord. My son had a very close relationship with the Lord through Jesus Christ."[137] The girl who Bert was dating wrote in her journal about her conversations with Bert: "I thought about Bert and the times that both he and I would discuss God, and how we wanted tangible, visible evidence of God's existence and his working power in our lives."[138] When Joy Ellis called home and asked her parents to pray about who she would choose as her homecoming escort, she told them that she wanted to select someone who had an exemplary Christian faith.[139] It's no wonder she chose Bert Rapp.

It seems likely that Bert would have followed his father into the world of banking and finance in New York City. A classmate mused: "What a great addition he would have been. He wouldn't have been a greedy, in-it-for-himself businessman."[140] A work supervisor and friend noted Bert's desire to "quietly but forcefully change the injustices of society."[141] A business professor commented that "Bert was on a great path, both spiritually and in his career," and a fellow business student said "Bert would have been a success at anything he would have chosen in his career."[142] During summer vacations, Bert worked at the Hudson City Savings Bank in Paramus, New Jersey, and was described by a bank executive as "an outstanding individual."[143]

Bert once brought a classmate home with him to New Jersey, and the two friends spent a day together sightseeing in New York City. The classmate remembers the indisputable highlight of the day as meeting Bert's father for lunch in a private dining room at the Bank of New York. It was a heady experience for Bert's friend from a small town in rural western New York—a skyscraper, an executive dining room, an elegant meal—each course summoned when Mr. Rapp pressed a button on the table. What made the luncheon so impactful, though, was the opportunity to see the obvious pride Mr. Rapp had in the extraordinary young man his son was becoming.[144]

Mr. Rapp's namesake was so beloved and respected on campus that the classmate who shared a room with him for three years said: "I don't think anybody ever said a bad word about Bert. I only knew him for three years, but I will never forget him. I don't think anyone would ever forget being friends with Bert Rapp."[145]

— CINDY RUDES —

A stereotypical image of Christian missionaries pictures intrepid evangelists and Bible translators who travel to a faraway land, don pith helmets, chop their way through remote jungles, and traverse uncharted waterways in dugout canoes in order to share Christ with those who have never heard of him. As pioneer missionaries with the Christian and Missionary Alliance denomination, Raymond and Ruth Rudes did exactly that—on the island of Borneo in Indonesia. After serving for fifteen years in a field station they built from scratch, Mr. Rudes' responsibilities expanded into writing and publication, and the couple moved to the city of Bandung on the island of Java, where their first daughter, Debbie, was born. Cindy was born the next year, on September 9, 1960, while the family was home on furlough in her father's hometown of Genoa, Ohio. The family returned to Indonesia shortly thereafter. While in elementary school, Cindy and Debbie lived at home and attended a nearby school for missionary kids. The transition to middle and high school, though, required a move to the Dalat boarding school in faraway Malaysia. Cindy and Debbie would be at Dalat for four months in the fall, home for two months at Christmas, back to Dalat for four months in the spring, and then home for two months in the summer. Other than her ninth-grade year, which her family spent on furlough in Maryland, Cindy's high school education was completed at Dalat, and she graduated in 1978.

Despite the many miles between Cindy and her parents for most of those years, she and Debbie knew they were deeply loved. Mr. and Mrs. Rudes wrote their daughters multiple letters a week, each one filled with expressions of love and assurances that they were missed. Cindy and Debbie would frequently read these letters to their classmates who didn't receive as many letters from home. Visits home at Christmas and in the summer included as much time as possible with their parents and ended with a trip to the airport where Mr. and Mrs. Rudes would cry openly as they sent their daughters back to school.

Debbie remembers Cindy as "the funny one"—always bringing her sense of humor and keen enjoyment of life to any endeavor. As little girls, they frequently played outside, pretending they were pioneer girls and emulating what their parents had done in the jungles of Borneo. In high school, they played every possible sport together—basketball, tennis, softball, and volleyball. With their parents so far away—and unable to communicate with them other than by letters that could take a week or more to arrive—the two girls had to parent and mentor one another. If the two sisters squabbled, Mrs. Rudes would say to them, "You need to stick together, because someday we're not going to be here. But you'll always have each other."[146]

Cindy was one of several Dalat graduates who came to Houghton College in the late 1970s. Anticipating that she would return to Indonesia as a missionary upon graduation, Cindy became a communications major with minors in Bible and history. "Her heart's desire was to return and serve God there [Indonesia] in whatever way she could."[147] Her desire to return to the mission field was a logical expression of her deep commitment to her Christian faith. As one friend wrote: "God was the key to her. Her relationship with Christ meant everything. Christ was someone she lived with personally every day and shared with anyone who would listen. She was always so ready to share what God had been doing for her. He always provided for her needs, and she assured us he would do the same for us."[148] Cindy's deep faith was evident to her friends and classmates at Houghton, as her senior year she served as chaplain of the senior class and led the weekly class prayer meeting.[149]

Cindy cherished her Indonesian heritage, and her multicultural upbringing provided her with unique opportunities to make people laugh. She would say certain phrases in Indonesian, and when her friends would pretend to speak Indonesian in return, an animated "conversation" would ensue that inevitably ended with everyone laughing.[150] She enjoyed eating Indonesian dried fruit treats that her parents sent. These treats had an unusual taste to the American palate, so Cindy would get a kick out of offering them to people as "candy" and then watching their face contort with unpleasantness. "She loved to torture people with her candy."[151] When her sister Debbie called on the phone, Cindy would sometimes switch into the Indonesian language, and her roommates would say, "Are you talking about us?" Cindy would laugh and say, "No, we've got better things to be talking about than you guys!" With a twinkle in her eyes and a smile on her face, "Cindy could walk in the room and have everyone laughing within minutes."[152] "She made life fun for those around her."[153]

Even Dr. Chamberlain, the president of the college, was fair game for Cindy's lighthearted humor. As senior class chaplain, she asked Dr. Chamberlain to join the senior class for their fall retreat. In a subsequent conversation, she clarified for Dr. Chamberlain what his assignment at the retreat would be. Before the second conversation, she wrote in a letter to her parents that she needed to speak with the president again "to be sure he knows what he's doing"—a comment she punctuated with a smiley face.[154]

On the women's volleyball team, Cindy (known as "Ruders" among her teammates) was a spiker who played on the front row. She was not the star player but was a hard worker who always encouraged her teammates.[155] Two teammates recalled that Cindy happily turned a cartwheel at every practice and game and was known to sing Indonesian lullabies to teammates who weren't feeling well. They poked fun at her "light feet that sounded like a herd of thundering buffalo."[156] The team sang together on van rides to and from away games, and Cindy always wanted the windows open so everyone could wave their arms in unison while singing "Love is a flag flown high from the castle of my heart."[157] When the team van had a minor collision with a cow on the way back to campus after a game, Cindy laughed and laughed and was eager for more excitement.[158] But she knew when to be serious, too. Her coach remembers how focused she was on her studies, squeezing homework into every available minute.[159] Her teammates wrote: "Cindy was a spiritual leader. She never failed to thank God for the talent he had given her and was always praising him no matter what happened."[160] Her teammates honored her for the many ways in which she demonstrated leadership on the team by selecting her as a captain senior year.

Cindy was energetic and upbeat, full of life; one friend described her as "sparkly."[161] Another as "vivacious."[162] But she was also "grounded and mature, she knew who she was."[163] And she loved people. A younger member of the volleyball team who was also new to the sport remembers how Cindy reached out to her and made her feel welcome on the team.[164] Her roommate remembers: "Cindy was such a treat to be around, so enjoyable, so personable. You could tell her anything. You always had her full attention. She would say, 'Let's pray about it,' and we'd pray together. Then we'd go get ice cream in the snack shop."[165] She participated in a group that provided support to missionary kids.[166] She missed her family in Indonesia, and as a surrogate, she kept in her room a well-worn teddy bear named for her father, Ray.[167]

Thanks to the generosity of a family friend, Cindy and her sister Debbie were able to spend a few weeks in the summer of 1980 visiting their parents in Indonesia. Cindy wrote an article, published posthumously by the denominational magazine of the Christian and Missionary Alliance, describing her departure from Indonesia at the end of the trip. She wrote of her gratitude to God for the generosity that made the trip possible: "I had prayed that I might be able to return to the land where I had grown up, and it was by miracles that God had answered my prayers." She described her love for her home country— the flowers, the food, the smells, the language. Most poignantly, though, she spoke of the pain of saying farewell to her beloved parents—the tears and hugs as they said good-bye, the pocket watch her father gave her as a keepsake of the trip, searching the crowd for one more glimpse of her parents as the airplane taxied down the runway before takeoff. Cindy finally picked her parents out of the many people waving good-bye; it turned out to be the last time she ever saw them: "They weren't just waving. Their arms were stretched out as they swayed back and forth. Their arms reached out to us, and somehow they seemed to reach around the world. Love would be stronger than any distance."[168]

THE SIX

"It's difficult to get six finer students together," said the academic dean at the time.[169] Between them, the members of Houghton's 1981 homecoming court touched virtually every organization and person on the close-knit Houghton campus. They were athletes, musicians, captains, senators, class presidents, organization presidents, chaplains, ministry volunteers, chapel partners, classmates, and roommates. The Six came from different points on the globe and different types of families. They possessed a wide array of interests, passions, and skills, and were heading into different professions—law, music, education, missions, and business. But each member of this group—Mark, Beth, Alan, Joy, Bert, and Cindy—possessed a deep and radiant Christian faith. Each one was accomplished in the classroom and in campus life. Each one was a prominent student leader. Each one was admired by a campus, loved by a wide circle of friends, and cherished by a devoted family back home. Each one was full of almost unimaginable promise. And each one got into the same car on the morning of October 2, 1981.

MILIEU

For years, Houghton's alumni magazine was called *Milieu* (or *Mildew,* for those with an irreverent bent). A milieu is a context or setting, and the milieu for the Houghton accident is provided in part by a particular place and time.

First, the place. Houghton College is a small Christian liberal arts college that is situated on a beautiful, wooded campus in rural western New York. Located on a plateau and hillside that overlooks the village of Houghton and the Genesee River valley, the campus was home to approximately 1,200 undergraduate students in 1981. "The quad" was the center of campus—a spacious rectangular lawn that hosted spirited games of ultimate frisbee in the fall, ice sculpture contests in the winter, and relaxing gatherings and conversations all year round. Surrounding the quad were several of the main campus buildings: the Luckey Administration Building, the Willard J. Houghton Library, the Woolsey and Fancher classroom buildings, the Reinhold Campus Center, a large women's residence called East Hall, the music building, and Wesley Chapel, the 1200-seat auditorium where the community gathered for chapel and other major events. The Paine Science Center, three other residence halls, and the physical education center were located at varying distances further away from the quad. Around the perimeter of the campus were athletic fields, the "ski slope" (generously named), and an extensive network of wooded trails that wound their way through the forests on college property. Sprinkled throughout the area around the campus were homes in which faculty, staff, and other community members lived. Juniors and seniors were given the option of moving off-campus and renting rooms in some of these homes.

The main street of the tiny village of Houghton was readily accessible via a short walk or drive down the hill. The village was anchored by the Houghton Wesleyan Church, which served as the de facto campus church. Several homes and a variety of small establishments lined the main road, including the Houghton Inn, a gas station, and the Pizza Barn. The nearest grocery store was four miles away in the neighboring village of Fillmore, and the nearest large town was Olean, a forty-five-minute drive from campus. For a trip to the big city, students drove to Buffalo or Rochester, both a little more than one hour away.

The time was 1981, which began with the inauguration of President Ronald Reagan in January. Reagan's landslide victory over incumbent Jimmy Carter was catalyzed by his promises to rebuild the nation's military and strengthen the struggling economy. Within minutes of his inauguration, Iran released fifty-two American hostages who had been held for 444 days. On March 30, John Hinckley Jr. attempted to assassinate Reagan in a deranged effort to impress the teenage movie star Jodie Foster. Six weeks later, Pope John Paul II survived an assassination attempt in Vatican City.

Trends and technologies that would shape the 1980s and beyond began to appear in 1981. NASA's space shuttle era began with the launch of *Columbia* in April. The AIDS virus was first identified in June. MTV began broadcasting in August, and about the same time, IBM released its first personal computer. Sandra Day O'Connor took her seat in September as the first woman to serve on the United States Supreme Court.

Some 750 million people around the world watched "the wedding of the century" as Prince Charles and Lady Diana Spencer exchanged vows on July 29. *Raiders of the Lost Ark*, starring a young Harrison Ford, was the summer movie blockbuster. Larry Bird and Magic Johnson were in the early stages of their budding rivalry in the National Basketball Association, while an aging Mohammad Ali lost his final boxing match and retired.

The Official Preppy Handbook was released in 1980, and Izod polo shirts with upturned collars were increasingly prevalent on college campuses by 1981. Disco fever had abated by the late 1970s, and the airwaves of the early 1980s were filled with hits by Styx, Genesis, Michael Jackson, and the Rolling Stones. Christian contemporary music was still in its infancy, and Houghton's radio station, WJSL, featured tunes by Phil Keaggy, Amy Grant, Keith Green, and Andrae Crouch. TV shows could only be viewed at the times prescribed by the three major networks, and top choices included *Dallas*, *M*A*S*H*, and *The Jeffersons*. America's evening news anchorman, Walter Cronkite, signed off for the final time on March 6.

Median family income in the United States was $22,390, and the median price of a home was $68,900. Minimum wage was $3.35 an hour. A year of tuition, room, and board at Houghton College cost $5,775.[1]

Technologies that are ubiquitous today were unheard of at the time—email, cell phones, laptops, the internet, social media. College professors used chalkboards and overhead projectors. Term papers were written on typewriters. Automobiles lacked safety features such as airbags, blind spot monitoring, and collision avoidance systems. Wearing seatbelts was neither mandated nor common.

THE CRASH

With only a week to go, preparations for the homecoming festivities were in full swing. For the six senior members of the homecoming court, those preparations included a quick trip together to Buffalo to pick up the Western-themed rental costumes they would wear. We have only a few glimpses into the activities and movements of the six seniors in the final handful of hours before they made that trip on Friday morning.

On Thursday, the group met with senior class president Allen Hemayakian to finalize the plans and budget for their trip to Buffalo.[2] Women's choir practice was held on Thursday, and Beth spoke excitedly to the student next to her about the Friday outing to Buffalo.[3] True to form, Bert acknowledged to a close friend that it was highly unusual and somewhat guilt-inducing for him to be skipping classes for a non-academic trip.[4] Mark joined Beth in the campus center for dinner, while she nursed what appeared to be the beginnings of a cold.[5]

Al spent Thursday evening at the Pizza Barn, where he mingled with friends and customers and closed out the night by helping his brother Warren take care of a bees' nest in the building.[6] Friday morning he had breakfast in the campus center and then had an appointment with Professor Ruth Hutton at 9:45 a.m.[7] He was to rehearse for her a poetry reading that he would be presenting in her Oral Interpretation class the following Monday, but Professor Hutton's earlier meeting ran late and she asked if he would mind waiting a few minutes. "I wouldn't mind, but some other students are waiting for me to go with them to Buffalo," Al responded. "We have to pick up our costumes for homecoming next weekend. I should be back early afternoon. Maybe I can see you then."[8]

Cindy spent Thursday evening at volleyball practice and led devotions for the team from her favorite psalm—Psalm 144.[9] Perhaps she read these words from that psalm to her friends: "Lord, what are human beings that you care for them, mere mortals that you think of them? They are like a breath; their days are like a fleeting shadow" (Ps. 144:3–4). Like Al, Cindy left campus Friday morning with plans to reconnect with someone later that day. While still in bed that morning, she was chatting with her roommate Marlene Gifford and said, "Mar, we need to go to dinner sometime soon. We haven't really talked in a long time. We need to go to dinner, just the two of us."[10] The plan was set, without either imagining that those would be the last words they would ever say to one another.

Mark had breakfast in the campus center with the Student Senate president, Susan Facer, to discuss their shared project of revising the constitution for the college radio station, WJSL. They made plans for a lunch meeting that Susan would lead later in the day without Mark due to his trip to Buffalo.[11]

Beth met her housemate and fellow flute major, Mercy, on the quad that morning and asked Mercy to hold on to her flute while she made the quick trip to Buffalo. The flute's owner was Beth's flute instructor, who played with the Rochester Philharmonic Orchestra and had loaned it to Beth for her upcoming senior recital. Mercy took the flute, and the two close friends exchanged a hug and agreed to meet for dinner in the campus center that evening.[12]

Bert was beginning to date a girl in the junior class named Karyn, and the two of them saw each other at breakfast. They chatted a little about Bert's trip to Buffalo and made plans to get together that evening. Karyn was excited to see Bert that evening, as she was planning to tell him that she "really liked him and wanted to date him for sure."[13]

The exact composition of the group making the trip seems to have been uncertain until Friday morning. The senior class president, Allen Hemayakian, was originally planning to join The Six for the trip but decided that he needed more time to prepare for a Friday afternoon exam. He called one of The Six that morning, excused himself from the trip, and told them to go ahead without him.[14] Bert had invited another friend to come along; perhaps others had as well.[15] A group of seven or more would have required a larger vehicle—or more likely, the group would have split into two cars.

At some point, it became clear that only the six members of the homecoming court would be making the trip, and they decided to go in Mark's blue, four-door Volkswagen Dasher. One or two of the young men went to the Student Senate office, which adjoined the campus center lounge, to pick up the check they would use to pay for the costume rentals.[16] A friend saw Al and Cindy together in the campus center lounge, waiting for the rest of the group, so it appears the lounge was the rendezvous point where the group met.[17] Once all six were together, they likely exited the campus center on the side away from the quad, since a convenient drive-up lane was located just outside that entrance on Genesee Street. Given the approximately fifty-five-minutes drivetime from campus to the accident site, it must have been about 10:00 a.m. when they piled into Mark's car and pulled away from the campus center. It was a drizzly, chilly morning as the six friends drove down the hill toward the village, turned onto Route 19A next to the Houghton College sign and across from the Houghton Wesleyan Church, and left town for the final time. In spite of the gloomy weather, one imagines them in high spirits as they begin a thank-God-it's-Friday road trip with friends to the nearest big city, in anticipation of an approaching homecoming weekend that would surely be a highlight of their senior year.

About sixty miles away in Angola, New York, a small town southwest of Buffalo on the shores of Lake Erie, a truck driver named Mr. Matthew

Bingenheimer had already started his day.[18] By the time the six students left campus, the fifty-one-year-old man, with a wife named Joan and four children, made the forty-five-minute drive from his home to the Fisher Price plant in East Aurora to pick up his next load. It was to be a routine delivery of toys and toy parts to Fisher Price's Medina plant—a trip of less than an hour, east on Route 20A, through the hamlet of Wales Center, then north on 77. Mr. Bingenheimer would have easily made his delivery to Medina in time for lunch, and then perhaps he would have gotten an early start on his weekend plans.

What transpired between the students' departure from campus and their arrival at the intersection of Routes 78 and 20A in Wales Center is left almost completely to our imagination. We know that the three couples were seated in the Volkswagen Dasher in a way that would be expected for two dating couples and one friend couple.[19] Mark, wearing jeans and a rust-colored shirt, was behind the wheel. Mark's girlfriend Beth, wearing a white sweater and blue pants, sat next to him in the front middle. Joy, wearing a green sweater, sat on the other side of Beth, next to the passenger door in the front seat. In the back seat, Alan sat directly behind Mark on the driver's side, wearing a blue sweatsuit with a red checked shirt. Cindy, in a bright yellow jacket, sat next to Alan in the middle. Bert sat on the other side of Cindy, directly behind Joy on the passenger side, attired in a blue shirt with a blue and white sweater. The compact car was full.

They could have chosen any number of routes to get to Buffalo, but all would have taken them through a western New York tapestry of small towns, rolling hills, forests, and farms. The location of the accident tells us they must have been traveling north on Route 78 at Java Village, and from there would have continued northwest for about ten miles through the hamlets of Strykersville and Wales Center before arriving at the crossroads with Route 20A. A journalist from Joy's hometown of Watertown, New York, retraced these final miles of their journey in the days after the accident and provided this description: "Their last seconds passed along a nondescript country road, up a steep hill, past a 'Re-Elect Ressler for Assessor' sign, past two weeping willows, and a yellow sign warning 'Stop Ahead.'"[20]

A classmate imagined what those final miles and minutes might have been like: "What did they talk about? Were they deeply involved in a theological debate—they were Houghton students after all. Or was it a mock-serious argument about the most demanding sport—volleyball versus soccer, perhaps? Did they have music on? Did Joy vote for Amy Grant while Mark pushed for Resurrection Band? Did Alan and Beth sing? Did Bert sit quietly watching out the window? Did Cindy re-tell the story of the volleyball van and the cow? Or maybe they were planning a skit for the Senate Spot scheduled Saturday evening of homecoming weekend, wherein Josh Randall, Hoss Cartwright, and Lucas McCain were to rescue the sweethearts of the rodeo and bring justice and peace to the Houghton Corral. A farmer standing by the roadside, morning mail in hand, seeing them zip by splashing up rooster tails of mist, would have smiled and thought, 'Good to be young.'"[21]

The intersection toward which the 1980 Volkswagen Dasher drove northwest on Route 78 and the 1979 GMC tractor-trailer drove east on Route 20A was notorious for its treachery. Numerous accidents had occurred there, at least two of them fatal.[22] As Route 78 approached the juncture with Route 20A from the south, it curved to the left (west), creating a Y-shaped intersection that gave the appearance of one road gently merging into the other. Two residents who lived nearby commented that the intersection created an optical illusion that often prompted drivers on Route 78 to think they could proceed through, even with a stop sign present.[23] Ron Becker, the chief of the Wales Center Volunteer Fire Company at the time, remembers that the tricky intersection created problems for many drivers who would miss the stop sign and "drive right on through."[24] The danger of the unusually shaped intersection was further complicated by several other factors: eastbound traffic on Route 20A tended to be going faster at this spot due to the intersection's location at the bottom of a hill; sightlines for drivers on Route 78 approaching the intersection were poor; the speed limit on both roads was 55 miles per hour; and there was no overhead traffic light marking the intersection. Some locals called it "Suicide Corner."[25]

And, on the morning of October 2, it was raining.

The collision occurred at 10:54 a.m.[26] Law enforcement officials reported that the Volkswagen Dasher failed to stop at the intersection and was consequently broadsided by the Fisher Price tractor-trailer heading downhill on Route 20A eastbound. It was a direct hit on the driver's side of the car. The impact was so strong that the car was crushed under the front of the truck's cab and pushed approximately 200 feet. The mangled car finally came to rest, pinned between the front of the truck and a two-foot-wide elm tree in the front lawn of a house on the north side of Route 20A. The six students were killed instantly. "They probably didn't even see it coming," commented one police officer.[27]

Mr. Melvin Kohn, owner of the home where the car came to rest, was hanging a plant inside the front window of his house. He heard the crash and looked up to see the truck pushing the car toward his house, ultimately ramming it into the tree just a short distance from where he stood. "It made a tremendous noise; for a moment, I thought it was going to come through the house."[28] "If it wasn't for that tree, that car and truck would have been in my living room!" Kohn exclaimed.[29] "It sounded like all hell was breaking loose."[30]

Mr. Kohn immediately called the fire department and then rushed outside to assist. He reported that a woman stopped her car right away and called out, "I'm a trained nurse!" She checked the wreckage and informed him that no one had survived.[31] Five of the bodies were found inside the car; one was lying on the ground just outside.[32] The first emergency personnel arrived at 10:59 a.m., and Mr. Kohn assisted them in directing traffic around the accident. Mr. Norman Seiflein, an assistant first aid captain with the Wales Center Fire Department reported that his unit was the first on the scene. He radioed for help and other departments quickly arrived. Seiflein commented: "We're not doctors, we're laymen, but we checked the people for signs of life and found none. We performed first aid procedures and got no response."[33]

The impact of the shattering collision was so overwhelming that Erie County sheriff Kenneth J. Braun commented, "You couldn't even tell what kind of car it was. It was just a tangled mess of steel and iron."[34] Rescue personnel worked for more than an hour to cut through the wreckage and remove the bodies.[35] All six were pronounced dead at the scene by Dr. Liu of the Erie County Medical Examiner's Office, and their bodies were transported away to the county morgue. Fire Chief Becker reported that the scene was "chaos for quite a while," as roads and intersections in the immediate vicinity had to be shut down and traffic redirected.[36]

One of the cars directed around the scene in the early moments was driven by Houghton philosophy professor Larry Mullen. In addition to his duties at the college, Professor Mullen was the part-time pastor at a small church and was on his way to Buffalo to visit a hospitalized parishioner. As he drove north on Route 78, following the same route the six students had traveled moments earlier, he came to the same intersection and saw "ambulances, fire trucks, and police cars everywhere." He saw the terror of the scene and felt compassion for whoever was involved but would not learn until several hours later that the victims were students at his own college.[37]

Sheriff Braun reported that the accident was the deadliest crash in Erie County history.[38] "I can't recall when we've ever had six killed in one vehicle. I've seen a lot of carnage in my life," he said. "I've been in this business 30 years and I fought as a Marine in the South Pacific, but this is one of the worst things I have ever seen. Just think about the families of these young people."[39] Fire Chief Becker also described the scene as the worst he had ever seen: "Everybody was shaken up by it."[40] Mr. Bingenheimer, the driver of the truck, suffered minor injuries and was taken to South Buffalo Mercy Hospital for examination. He was released later in the day, but offered no comment as his wife said he was "too shaken to discuss it."[41]

Mr. Kohn was unable to estimate how fast the truck may have been traveling, since he saw the truck only as it was slowing and coming to a stop. Authorities said there was no indication of excessive speed and no charges against the truck driver were filed. Mr. Kohn was deeply affected by all he had seen: "Maybe you people [the media] will be able to do something about this dangerous intersection now. We've been yelling for years, but the Town Board said it's a state highway and they [the town] can't do anything. We need a speed zone [the limit is now 55 mph], and we need a traffic light. It's just a shame those young people had to die like that."[42]

What actually led to the crash? Were The Six engaged in an animated conversation that distracted the driver? Was there some sort of mechanical issue, such as a faulty window defogger or broken windshield wiper? Did the gentle curve of the intersection cause them to miss the stop sign or approach it too quickly? Did another vehicle obstruct their view? Were they focused on something to their right and so failed to look back to the left? Did an animal dart into the road? Did the rain suddenly intensify? In this pre-GPS era, were they trying to read a map or written directions? Or is there some other explanation altogether? The answer went to the grave with them. The police report is stark in its brevity: "Vehicle #2 failed to yield right of way and was struck by vehicle #1."[43]

A surprise birthday party for one of the county's top deputy sheriffs was scheduled to start at noon at a restaurant in the Buffalo suburb of Cheektowaga. The party couldn't begin, though, because the organizer and host of the party was running late. Guests were beginning to make jokes about "the soup getting cold and the ice cubes melting in the water glasses" when Sheriff Braun finally walked into the banquet room. It was now well past noon, and Braun was quick to apologize to the gathered guests: "I'm sorry. You shouldn't have waited." And then his voice trailed off, becoming inaudible. He had been in law enforcement for twenty-five years and had seen combat as a Marine. He had just come from the scene of the accident, and as he stood in front of his colleagues, he wept.[44] The sheriff's tears were among the first of many that day.

SHOCK WAVES

The phone call came to campus at 1:45 p.m. Until that moment, it had been a typical Friday on campus—classes, labs, lessons, homework, chapel. One o'clock classes were winding down, and members of the cafeteria staff were cleaning up from the lunch rush. Students were making their Friday night plans or thinking about their trip home for the weekend. One phone call from the Erie County Sheriff's Office set in motion the shockwaves that shattered the normalcy and tranquility.

Robert Danner was the new dean of student development; he had just moved his family into their home near campus and started his role in July. He was a mere five weeks into his first academic year and, at this juncture, knew few students and little of how Houghton worked. Since President Daniel Chamberlain was traveling for the college in the New York City area, the call came to Danner's office, located in the campus center, just down a short hallway from where the six seniors had met less than four hours earlier. Danner was meeting with Kenneth Nielsen, the college treasurer, when his administrative assistant leaned in his office door. "I'm sorry to interrupt," she said, "but you'd better take this call. It's the Erie County Sheriff." When Bob Danner picked up the phone, he became the first person on the Houghton campus to learn what had happened and who had died. He responded to the news with disbelief: "You mean all six are gone!"[45]

Danner and Nielsen walked quickly around the quad to Nielsen's office in the Luckey Administration Building, where they were joined by Dr. Fred Shannon, academic dean. The three campus leaders, without their president, without a playbook, and with their own shock and grief to manage, undoubtedly bowed their heads for a moment of prayer, set aside all other projects and priorities, and then began to respond to the tragedy. "We went to work, and we had to work quickly."[46]

The first priority was to coordinate with the sheriff's office and other law enforcement officials in the dreadful task of notifying next of kin—no small challenge with families spread from Pennsylvania to Indonesia and a handful of immediate family members who were students at Houghton or lived in the community. The group knew that a pastoral presence would be critical, so Dr. Shannon called Rev. Mark Abbott, the pastor of the Houghton Wesleyan Church. Abbott was working in his office down in the village that morning. When he picked up his phone, Fred Shannon asked if he could come to the Luckey building on campus immediately, without providing any further explanation. Abbott made the short drive up the hill to campus, reversing the drive the six students had made earlier that morning, and walked into Shannon's office. There he found Danner, Nielsen, and Shannon—"three somber-faced administrators"—who told him the news. Abbott reflected on his initial response: "How could this be? Just one student killed in a closely knit college community is a major tragedy. But six! The whole senior homecoming court!"[47]

The four now began working together with the authorities to notify the parents and siblings of The Six. While Abbott, Nielsen, and Shannon provided Houghton knowledge and connections, Danner's military background enabled him to bring a specialized and valuable skill. He had previously worked with a military unit called "casualty reporting"—the military officers who bring the dreaded "knock on the door" to the homes of soldiers who have been killed, notify the loved ones, and walk with the family through the first days of grieving. Danner commented: "Because of some previous history at the college,

I came to Houghton trying to hide my military background. But that part of my background helped us on that particular day."[48]

The team worked feverishly to find names, addresses, and phone numbers of parents. A staff member in the registrar's office remembers Danner coming to their office "looking just as gray as I had ever seen anyone look. He could barely speak." He asked where the student information files were and then sat at an empty desk for quite some time, pulling out files and writing down notes. His only explanation was, "There's been an accident."[49] Shannon remembers the group having lengthy conversations with a variety of law enforcement agencies and officials, exchanging information and trying to coordinate the notification process so that it would be done as efficiently and with as much compassion as possible.[50] Whenever feasible, contact was made with the pastors of the students' respective home churches so the family pastor could also be present when the news was delivered.[51]

Concurrent with all these efforts to notify the families, President Chamberlain also needed to be informed. He was scheduled to board a plane in New York City that afternoon for his return flight to western New York, arriving back on campus later that evening. Danner called the airport and was finally able to speak with someone who was able to arrange for Dr. Chamberlain to be paged. Just as he was about to board, he heard: "Daniel Chamberlain. Daniel Chamberlain. Please come to the nearest service counter for a message." Chamberlain was startled to hear his name coming over the airport loudspeakers and rushed to take the call. He wrote: "The message was terse: 'Please call your office immediately!' The plane I now feared I would miss was taking me back home, to upstate New York. In three short hours, I would have been there. What could possibly have happened that couldn't wait for my arrival? What could be the surprise on the other end of the line?"[52]

The surprise was more than Houghton's president could have imagined. When he called into his office, Bob Danner took the call and gave him the news of six students killed in a car accident. Chamberlain's plane was now boarding, so there was no time even to get the names of The Six. "I'll phone you from Rochester to get more facts. I've got to run, or the plane will leave without me."[53] The shaken president made his way to his window seat and spent the flight looking at the horizon, wondering who the students might be, pondering the enormity of the loss for the families and the community, and thinking about how he could best serve and guide a grief-stricken community.

Families began to receive the news. Pastor Abbott was dispatched to personally notify immediate family members who attended the college or lived in town, hopefully reaching them before the news began to break more generally. Joy Ellis' younger brother Don was a freshman at the college and lived in Shenawana Dorm, a men's residence which was a short walk up a hill from the administration building. Resident director Tim Nichols saw Pastor Abbott as he approached the front door and knew from Abbott's countenance that something was horribly wrong; he appeared "shattered." Abbott informed Nichols that he needed to speak with Don Ellis and asked where his room was located. Nichols presumed that something must have happened to Joy but had no information. Abbott seems to have believed that Nichols had already been informed, as he simply said: "I can't believe they're all gone." As the two men walked together down one flight of stairs to Don's lower-level room, Nichols offered to accompany Abbott into the room. Abbott thought it would be better if just one person delivered the news, so Tim waited outside in the hallway as the community's pastor informed a young man not yet twenty years old that his older sister had just been killed.[54]

Warren and Barbara Bushart, Al's brother and sister-in-law, were working at the Pizza Barn, preparing for what would surely be a large Friday night crowd of happy, hungry college students and community members. The Busharts were listening, as they frequently did, to radio station WKBW out of Buffalo. They began hearing news reports of a bad car accident in the Buffalo area that had left six people dead and wondered to each other, "What could have happened? Was it an entire family?" At about 3:00 in the afternoon, Barb had gone to a nearby parking lot to practice driving a stick-shift car. Warren looked out the window and saw Pastor Abbott walking up the driveway toward their front door, which was highly unusual, since Abbott was not a regular customer. When Barb came back a few minutes later, she saw Warren coming outside to meet her and knew immediately from his distraught expression that something was wrong. "What is it?" she asked. Warren shared the news that Abbott had shared with him: "That car accident on the radio wasn't a family; that was Al and Cindy and the rest of them."[55]

Moments later, their phone rang. Mrs. Bushart, Warren and Al's mother, was on the line and told them that the state police had just come to the family home and notified them of Al's death. All Warren and Barb could think of was to get home, so they quickly closed up the pizza shop, threw a few things in the car, and put a sign on the door that said, "Death in the family." Before pulling out of the driveway, Barb remembered that Alan probably didn't have any clothes back at his childhood home. She went to Al's closet and lovingly picked out one of the suits he wore when he sang with Son Touched, and the grieving young couple headed for home.[56]

Kevin Bushart, another of Al's brothers, was in his residence hall room at Lancaster Bible College when someone knocked on his door and told him he had a phone call. His mother's trembling voice was on the other end of the line, saying words he will never forget: "Al has been killed in an accident. You'd better try to find a way to get home." Kevin tried to ask questions, but his mother had little information at that point. "I remember feeling like I had been punched in the gut. I couldn't breathe."[57]

Mildred Rapp, Bert's mother, saw a police car drive up to her home in Harrington Park, New Jersey, about 3:00 p.m. When her pastor's car also pulled up, her thoughts immediately went to her husband, "never dreaming it was my son." She commented to a reporter: "I keep thinking about the driver of that truck and what he must be going through right now, knowing that he hit a car and killing six kids. And I just wish that I could help him and talk to him."[58]

Cindy Rudes' sister, Debbie, had just returned home from her position as a teacher at a small Christian school in West Virginia. She was washing dishes when her phone rang. Dr. Peter Nanfelt, an executive with the Christian and Missionary Alliance denomination, told her that her little sister had just died in a car accident. They spoke only very briefly, as Debbie was unable to continue the conversation. They agreed that he would call back in a few moments after Debbie had the opportunity to absorb the news, and when he did, he told Debbie that the authorities had not yet been able to locate her parents in Indonesia. Debbie remembered that they might be attending a conference together in Hong Kong and suggested they contact the denominational office there. Debbie and her boyfriend began making the trip to Genoa, Ohio, her father's hometown, where the family would begin gathering.[59]

Mr. and Mrs. Rudes were finally located in Hong Kong and notified of Cindy's death with this message from their supervisor: "Your daughter Cindy, with five other students from Houghton, were involved in an accident at 11:00 a.m. October 2 in Wales, New York, a suburb of Buffalo. They missed a stop sign and were hit broadside by a tractor-trailer truck, and all were killed. Cindy's body is now in the Erie County Hospital morgue in Buffalo."[60] The fact that Mr. and Mrs. Rudes were together in Hong Kong was extremely unusual; it was more typical for Mrs. Rudes to remain at home in Indonesia while her husband attended conferences such as this one. This time, however, Mr. Rudes had practically insisted that she accompany him. Had Mr. Rudes been in Hong Kong and Mrs. Rudes back in Indonesia, the logistics of their return to the United States would have been much more complex. As it was, they were able to obtain flights from Hong Kong to the United States and begin the long journey to their daughter's funeral.[61]

The police chief of Pottstown, Pennsylvania, was well acquainted with Mr. and Mrs. Andes, so he took it upon himself to knock on their door and give them the news.[62] Upon hearing of the accident, Gerald Andes, Beth's father, initially assumed that Beth must have been on her way to her flute lesson. "We thought at first that maybe she was going to Rochester because she took lessons there every week from the second-chair flutist in the Rochester symphony—but that's on Saturday."[63]

At some point while the families were beginning to receive the news, Dr. Chamberlain's flight arrived at the Rochester, New York, airport. "By the time the plane landed, I was nearly beside myself with the enormity, the finality, yet the incompleteness of the news I'd received."[64] His daughter, Priscilla, whose husband Mark was a medical student at the University of Rochester, picked him up at the airport. As soon as she saw him, she said: "Dad, you look white as a sheet! What happened? What's wrong?" He told her about the call he'd received in New York City, about six students lost in a terrible accident, and how urgently he needed to call the college to receive more information. They drove to her nearby apartment, where Dr. Chamberlain called Bob Danner and first learned the identities of The Six. "I had spent the whole flight wondering if I would know any of them, or one of them, or two of them. But as Bob went down the list, of course, I knew all six of them. They were our best. I was just stunned."[65]

In an almost unimaginable twist of irony, Dr. Chamberlain realized that a brother of one of the dead students was right there with them in his daughter's apartment. Dr. Keith Anderson, Mark's brother and a medical resident at the University of Rochester, had stopped over to visit with Priscilla's husband, Dr. Chamberlain's son-in-law. Dr. Chamberlain momentarily stopped his conversation with Danner to call out to Keith: "Please wait until I'm finished; I need to speak with you when I'm done." But Keith evidently thought Dr. Chamberlain's request was intended for his son-in-law, and by the time Chamberlain was off the phone, he had left the apartment to return to the hospital.[66] Keith was busily treating patients in the intensive care unit when he received word that he had a phone call. Dr. Chamberlain, who he had just seen, was on the phone. When Keith heard the news, all he could say to Dr. Chamberlain was "Are you sure?" Mark's death was "beyond fathoming." When Keith hung up the phone, a group of medical colleagues approached him with a question about a patient. Keith "couldn't really even hear them. I just sort of stared into space. I told them that my brother just died."[67] Keith called his brother Terry, who also lived in upstate New York, with the news and both began the drive home to Connecticut to be with their grieving parents. Unfortunately, the youngest of the four Anderson brothers, Kevin, was the only one at home when the police knocked on the front door, and so he was the one who had to break the news to Mark's parents.[68]

By mid-afternoon, the story of a car accident with six fatalities was being disseminated more broadly through the media. The names of the deceased had not yet been released publicly, pending notification of the next of kin, but the college administrators knew that would happen before long and understood the need to begin communication with the student body. Some media reports were evidently beginning to mention Houghton College, as Dr. Charles Massey, the dean of Houghton's West Seneca Campus in suburban Buffalo, remembers being contacted by media members on Friday afternoon looking for additional information. Many seemed to think that the West Seneca Campus *was* Houghton College; they were unaware of the rural campus in Allegany County.[69]

In those days, before email, cell phones, and social media, communicating sensitive information with accuracy and speed to 1200 undergraduates was no small challenge. The administrators decided to hold a campus-wide informational meeting in Wesley Chapel at 7:00 p.m. and began taking measures to spread the word that now seem almost quaint. Bob Danner walked back over to the Reinhold Campus Center, climbed onto a chair in the center of the lounge, and gathered as many students around him as possible. He told the students that there had been a serious car accident involving Houghton students and that the college would have more information to share at a meeting in Wesley Chapel that evening. He asked the students to spread the word about the meeting.[70] Printed notices with that same information were posted on doors in the Reinhold Campus Center and other buildings around campus.[71] Announcements went out over the residence hall intercoms.[72] Parents began calling the campus to confirm the safety of their own children, and students began lining up at dorm payphones to call home for the same purpose. And slowly, organically, unevenly, as one student told another, as radios and televisions were turned on, as conversations with parents unfolded, the unbelievable news began to spread through the campus. The details were still murky and sometimes conflicting: How many students? Who were they? Was it really the homecoming court? Were they all killed? But the extent of the tragedy was slowly becoming clearer.

By 5:00 p.m., news reports were identifying the students. Campus radio station WJSL followed suit at about 5:15 p.m., and for the first time, the college named publicly the six students whose names would forever be linked together in death: Mark Anderson, Beth Andes, Alan Bushart, Joy Ellis, Bert Rapp, and Cindy Rudes.[73] The small college was plunged into mourning, almost like being pushed into a walk-in freezer and made numb by the chill. Said one student at the time: "The campus became awfully quiet. Everywhere you looked there were just blank faces."[74]

Almost without exception, people who were in Houghton that afternoon still remember with precision where they were and what they were doing when the news came to them. It is impossible to put these vignettes into an exact chronological sequence, but they provide a picture of how the crushing news cascaded through the campus that Friday afternoon and evening.

Kathie Brenneman, a staff member at the college, had taken her twelve-year-old son to the Luckey Administration Building so that he could deliver newspapers there. When her son came back out to the car, he reported to Kathie, "Something awful has happened. The minister is in there. Something about an accident and college kids being killed." Kathie remembers it as "a horrifying feeling—the death of the innocents."[75]

Tim Nichols, the Shenawana resident director, was sitting in the room of a freshman student, providing some advance warning about a good-natured prank that was about to unfold. The conversation was interrupted by an all-dorm announcement, which alerted Tim to the fact that something was desperately wrong, since dorm announcements were supposed to be preapproved by him. The announcement was about the all-campus meeting in Wesley Chapel that evening. Tim ran down to the front desk of the residence hall, "shivering with anxiety," wondering who had authorized the announcement and what an all-campus meeting could possibly be about. Then he saw Pastor Mark Abbott approaching the front door to inform Don Ellis of the news, and while talking to him (in the conversation described earlier), he began to put the pieces together. Nichols reported, "Everything after that conversation is a haze to me. It's as though I was wandering around in a trance."[76]

Meg Martino, the Student Senate vice president, was near her office in the Reinhold Campus Center when she heard from a fellow student that the homecoming court had been in an accident and that "at least a couple are dead." Her initial response was to disbelieve the report, at least until it had been confirmed by a reliable source. When the news was confirmed later in the afternoon, Meg remembers "everyone in shock, crying and not knowing how to react."[77]

The men's soccer team had a light workout on Friday afternoon in final preparation for Saturday's game. Since Al was a captain and never missed practice, everyone on the team was asking, "Where's Al?" Some knew that he had gone to Buffalo with the homecoming group, but also knew that he should have been back by this time. Practice concluded, the players dispersed, and Coach Burke walked up the hill from the soccer field toward his office in the gymnasium. When he arrived at the top of the hill, near Shenawana residence hall, he saw Dr. Shannon waiting for him. Shannon said: "I have some bad news for you" and told him about the accident and Al's death. "I was devastated," Burke said.[78] Brian Davidson, Al's best friend and soccer co-captain had been very concerned about Al's absence at practice: "I knew something was wrong." He was in the gymnasium when he heard the news from men's basketball coach David Jack: "I cried in his arms for a long time."[79]

The women's volleyball team was also at practice. At first Coach Spurrier thought Cindy was late to practice, which was very surprising and somewhat frustrating with a big match coming up. In the middle of practice, Coach Spurrier was unexpectedly called away and asked the seniors to lead practice for a few minutes. When she returned, she was visibly shaken. She first called the seniors into the locker room and gave them the news; after a few moments the rest of the team came in as well. One team member recalls: "Everyone was crying. I didn't truly understand what was happening. We prayed and walked to campus in our own fogginess."[80]

The women's soccer team was at practice on the field when they were all called into the gymnasium for a team meeting. They gathered into one of the classrooms in the gymnasium and were informed of the accident by their coach. Jan Merz Kennedy recalls that the news created "an otherworldly, rock-your-world kind of shock." The team held each other close in a time of prayer, while Jan remembers thinking, "This can't be real, this can't be real."[81]

Mary Beth Fuller was in the campus center, having an impromptu meeting about homecoming with a couple of her classmates who had leadership roles in the planning. She noticed that her normally upbeat friends seemed quite somber, and they finally revealed that although they weren't sure of the details, something bad had happened. Later, Mary Beth and her roommate went to the snack bar in the lower level of the campus center where a television was showing the Buffalo news. As the announcers reported on the accident and provided the names of the deceased, Mary Beth screamed and collapsed into tears with her roommate. The two of them together made the short walk from the campus center back to their rooms in East Hall: "We were both just sobbing, wailing honestly." As they walked, they saw the men's soccer team walking slowly toward the campus center. They had clearly just been informed of the death of their co-captain, Alan, and the other five, and were "just as silent as could be."[82]

Karyn Hecht, who planned to tell Bert about her feelings for him that evening, was sitting on her bed in her dorm room, sewing a hem on a dress. She heard the news on her radio and gathered herself enough to walk down the hill to the home of Bert's sister and brother-in-law, who both worked in the college library and from whom Bert rented a room. She sat with them in their living room, all stunned. Among her many thoughts was the realization that she would never get to tell Bert the very thing he was hoping to hear from her.[83]

Professor Richard "Jake" Jacobsen had been playing racquetball in the gym and was walking back to his office when he heard the news.[84] Connie Finney was a staff member at the Buffalo campus where she was informed of the accident by Charles Massey: "It wasn't real to me. I was floored. I couldn't take it in. I walked around in a fog the rest of the day."[85] Becca Thorn was walking into her off-campus house after field hockey practice when she found out: "I just wanted to be alone and went to my room and crumpled to the floor."[86] Allen Hemayakian, who had missed the trip to Buffalo due to an afternoon exam, had completed the exam and was back in his assistant resident director's apartment when he received a phone call with the news: "The moment I got that call is like a photograph in my mind."[87]

Marlene Gifford and Betty Bowser lived in the same house as Cindy and Joy. They knew their two dear friends had taken the trip to Buffalo and remember thinking that they had been gone a long time and should have been back by now. The two were sitting in the living room of the house when one of the men's soccer players came to the door and asked Betty to come outside so he could speak with her alone. He then shared with her the news that had just been given to the soccer team. When they came back inside and told Marlene, she could not believe the news: "Is this true? Is this some kind of awful joke?" When he replied that it was true and all six had been killed, Marlene said that it "felt like I had just been hit. I can't begin to put into words what it felt like." Together, the three friends turned on the television news and watched in horror as the lead story showed pictures of the accident scene and yearbook photographs of their six lost friends. They went to the campus center to be with other friends and Marlene describes the scene: "I was literally shaking; we were just holding on to each other. People were like zombies, walking around in a daze." She remembers a friend running into the campus center crying out, "Is it true? Is it true?"[88] Sadly, it wasn't a rumor. Or a joke. Or a bad dream.

Mercy Zecher, with Beth's flute in her possession, was practicing in the music building throughout the afternoon. As dinnertime approached, she began to wonder why Beth hadn't come to the practice room so they could go to dinner together. She went to the music building lounge and asked other students if any of them had seen Beth. None of them had seen her, but their facial expressions were strained and one of them mentioned something about a bad car accident. Mercy immediately walked to the house near campus in which she, Beth, and two other girls rented rooms. When she walked in the front door, she noticed that the door into the living room of the woman who owned the house was open, which was unusual. Mercy's housemates and the landlord were watching the Buffalo television news, and the group opened their arms and folded Mercy into their tearful embrace.[89]

Many students learned the news while they were eating dinner in the campus center cafeteria. Brian Segool heard reports and rumors swirling around the campus that afternoon—rumors of a tragedy, rumors of an accident, rumors of death. As he ate dinner in the cafeteria with his then-girlfriend, the campus radio station was playing over the sound system, and he heard the deejay confirm the news of the accident and slowly read each of the six names. "It was surreal. It was one of the most unreal moments of my life. My girlfriend began to cry, and I held her hand but remember being unaware of what to say. What do you say? How do you feel?"[90] Erma Mekeel was also eating dinner when she heard the same announcement: "Forks dropped, eyes filled with tears, heads shook. Was it true? No one finished their meal."[91] When students left the cafeteria, they walked down the wooden stairs into the campus center lounge—which by this time was beginning to fill with students. Many gathered in small groups, crying, holding each other. Some went to Wesley Chapel to be alone and pray.

The spacious and casual lobby of East Hall, with its overstuffed sofas and fireplace, also became a gathering point for students. Mark Ohl entered the lobby, and it was "abuzz with activity. People were hugging and crying and yelling. I had no idea why." When he asked a friend what was happening, she said, "Haven't you heard? They're all gone!" and ran off crying.[92]

Those who had been off campus for the day quickly discovered that something was amiss when they returned. Professor Ruth Hutton reported that her son, a recent graduate, walked across campus late Friday afternoon hoping to reconnect with friends. However, instead of receiving the friendly smiles and waves that were typical of the Houghton community, "silent folk with red, swollen eyes looked down as he approached. The silence was eerie. From somewhere, he could hear subdued sobbing." Unable to discern what was wrong, he finally walked into the music building and asked if anyone knew what was happening. There he learned what the rest of the campus was finding out.[93]

Bert Rapp's best friend and roommate, Ed Taylor, had been student teaching in the nearby village of Perry that day. He returned to campus about 4:30 p.m. and was struck by the strange quiet in the campus center. He asked someone the question of the day—what's going on?—and when he heard the news, he thought, "That isn't true. That *can't* be true!" Confirmation came when his girlfriend told him about the reports she had seen on the television news. Ed dreaded the thought of returning to the room he had shared with Bert, where Bert's books and clothes and other possessions would be just as he had left them that morning, frozen in time.[94]

When Dr. Charles Massey of the Buffalo campus learned that Cindy Rudes was one of The Six, he mentioned to a journalist that Cindy and the women's volleyball team had been in a minor collision with a cow just the week before. Massey remembered laughing with Cindy about that incident at a soccer game earlier in the week. "She said they all stopped to see if everyone was okay, and then they laughed about it. Only the van's radiator was injured," he recalled. "Now," sighed Dr. Massey, rubbing his eyes, "it's all so ironic."[95]

The faculty of the Religion and Philosophy division gathered with their spouses for their monthly dinner at Turfside Restaurant in nearby Rushford. A restaurant employee came to their table and told them that the restaurant had received a call for Dr. Carl Schultz, who was professor of Old Testament and chair of the division. Dr. Schultz left the table to take the call and returned a few moments later to tell his colleagues that the six outstanding seniors had been killed. Dr. Harold Kingdon reported, "The shock was devastating." It wasn't long before Professor Larry Mullen returned from the hospital visit he had made in Buffalo and joined his colleagues at the restaurant. He saw immediately that the normally jovial group was "stunned and weepy" and asked what was wrong. When they told him that six Houghton students had been killed in a car accident in Buffalo, he flashed back: "I had no idea the accident I'd seen earlier was our own flesh and blood."[96]

After taking in the news, senior Graham Drake went back to his room and selected the song that would be the initial soundtrack to his mourning. Thinking mainly of his good friend Bert Rapp, but also of the other five, Graham listened over and over again to the popular 1970s song by the group Bread, called "Everything I Own." The song was written as a tribute to the songwriter's deceased father.[97] The lyrics capture the sentiment of the shattered Houghton community as an early autumn dusk began to settle over the campus:

> *And I would give anything I own*
> *I'd give up my life, my heart, my home*
> *I would give everything I own*
> *Just to have you back again.*[98]

GATHERING

At 7:00 p.m., the Houghton community—students, faculty and staff—gathered in Wesley Chapel to process, grieve, and pray. A reporter from the Buffalo News described the scene: "Heads were bowed in sorrow Friday night as a grief-stricken Houghton College community walked in a light rain to an informal memorial service to say goodbye to six seniors killed Friday morning in a Town of Wales car crash."[99] Student Dexter Davis had been off campus all afternoon refereeing a high school soccer game and returned to campus shortly before 7:00 p.m. He went to the gymnasium and was surprised to find nobody there: "It was a ghost town." Walking across campus toward the library, he walked by the chapel and saw what seemed to be the entire student body streaming in: "Lots of people and lots of tears."[100]

The main floor of the chapel was "full of shattered students, faculty, staff, and community members," with approximately 800 people in attendance.[101] At one point in the service, those who could not find seats were encouraged to come toward the front where seats were still available. Since the identities of the six deceased students had been public for nearly two hours now, most of the attendees "were seeking comfort, not information."[102] Many of those who were in Wesley Chapel that evening remember where they sat and who they sat with; I (Jack) was in the center section, about two-thirds of the way back, with a small group of my closest friends. Pastor Mark Abbott had taken the lead in planning the gathering, an unenviable task given the other responsibilities he fulfilled that afternoon, the brief time to prepare, and the magnitude of the occasion. He hoped the community could "take refuge in song and Scripture" in the informal service.[103] Robert Danner remembers the administration's desire that the service would "bring a sense of calmness and confidence in our faith."[104] President Chamberlain was still enroute back to campus and did not arrive in time to participate.

Fred Shannon, academic dean, opened the gathering with these words to the hushed crowd: "At this moment, you are probably nearly as fully informed as I regarding the nearly unbelievable tragic events of today. At 10:56 a.m. [sic] this morning, six of our students were killed instantly in an auto-truck collision in Erie County, some fifteen miles southeast of Buffalo. We have been in contact with the Erie County Sheriff's Department since approximately 1:30 this afternoon; that department has been in the process of notifying the parents or guardians. The six students were Mark Anderson, Beth Andes, Alan Bushart, Joy Ellis, Bert Rapp, and Cindy Rudes." After explaining President Chamberlain's absence, announcing that all weekend events were cancelled, and informing the campus of a formal memorial service in the coming days, Shannon read the first of dozens of telegrams that Houghton would receive: "The Nyack College community extends deepest sympathy to the Houghton College community in this tragedy. We pray for God's grace to keep you all under the mercy. Thomas P. Bailey, President of Nyack College."[105]

Pastor Abbott invited the community to "share together in the comfort of the Scriptures" and read portions of Psalm 90, James 4, and 2 Corinthians 1, including these excerpts:

> Lord, you have been our dwelling place throughout all generations. (Ps. 90:1)
>
> Now listen, you who say, "Today or tomorrow we will go to this or that city, spend a year there, carry on business and make money." Why, you do not even know what will happen tomorrow. What is your life? You are a mist that appears for a little while and then vanishes. (James 4:13–14)

> Praise be to the God and Father of our Lord Jesus Christ, the Father of compassion and the God of all comfort, who comforts us in all our troubles. (2 Cor. 1:3–4)

Abbott then prayed for God's comfort for the families and the community, while acknowledging the mysteries with which everyone was grappling: "Lord, we come into your presence this evening shocked and horrified. These have been good friends. These were beautiful people whose lives have been snuffed out, seemingly so tragically. And we experience questions, O God, and you permit us to ask, how could it happen? And why did it have to happen? We pray that you will draw our mind away merely from the questions and the horror of it all, to thanksgiving for the lives of those who did live among us. And for the memories we have."

Three student leaders offered brief comments and prayers. Student Senate president Susan Facer encouraged students to "unite in this grief" and reach out to one another and to faculty, staff, and administrators. Susan's opponent in the election for Senate president had been Mark Anderson, and she said of him: "I was just thinking this evening, as I was sitting in my office, at the desk that might have been Mark's, because he was equally qualified to hold that office, that if he were here right now, if he were to see me now, he would say 'Sue, go on, you can do it.' Because he was like that, he was always encouraging." Susan then thanked God for the lives of The Six, asked God to comfort the families, and grappled in her prayer with the tension between the loss and Christian hope: "Let us know that it's alright to feel hurt, it's alright to feel grief. But let us know equally as well that we can give those feelings to you and that you want them. Thank you for the victory of your servants. Thank you that their lives shone among us and that they are with you now."

Senior class president Allen Hemayakian reflected on the fact that his original plan would have had him in the car that morning: "For me personally, it's strange for me to think I could have been a part of that, and yet I'm not, and I'm here. And that's another 'Why?' that I am asking personally. But I do want to ask you, everyone, to trust the Lord—and not only be comforted, but try to comfort others."

Senior class chaplain Rick Dibble closed the student portion of the service with this prayer: "Our dear Lord God and heavenly Father, we come before you this evening and as has been said, we don't know how to pray. Lord, you are named in Scripture as the great Comforter; we need some of that comfort. You are named as the Prince of Peace; we need your peace. Father, we thank you for the fact that we can know that our fellow classmates are with you tonight. And they are rejoicing in your presence. Father, we pray that we would learn the lessons that you would have us learn from this experience. Help us to realize, Lord, that we can't count on the number of our days, that every day that we live is a gift from you, which we should live giving honor and glory to you. Lord, I pray that you will help those of us who are here at Houghton. We feel very much a part of these six students that have been taken away from us, but Father, I pray especially for their families. God, you know what it's like to be separated from your Son, who was your loved one. We just pray that you would comfort them and give them a peace in knowing that this is all in your will, your good and perfect will for us. We ask this in your name, believing. Amen."

Abbott then led the congregation in singing three hymns. The first, "It Is Well with My Soul," was written by Horatio Spafford after he learned of the deaths of his four daughters in a shipwreck. The Houghton congregation sang without the accompaniment of piano or organ: "When peace like a river attendeth my way, / when sorrows like sea billows roll, / whatever my lot, thou has taught me to say, / 'It is well, it is well with my soul.'"[106] Pastor Abbott then asked the congregation to join hands and "express in this tangible way our oneness with each other in this time of grief. And in a sense, we are one with those who have gone on because we are all part of the great mystical body of Christ." With hands joined across the chapel, the college community sang the hymn, "Blest Be the Tie That Binds": "We share our mutual woes, / our mutual burdens bear, / and often for each other flows / the sympathizing tear."[107] Finally, in what appears to have been a last-minute addition to the service, Abbott asked if someone was able to lead the congregation in singing a song that Al Bushart had recently sung in chapel: "Through It All." After a brief pause, a woman's voice led the community in the song that was popularized by Andrae Crouch: "I've had many tears and sorrows, I've had questions for tomorrow . . . but through it all, I've learned to trust in Jesus."[108]

The twenty-six-minute service ended with Pastor Abbott inviting everyone to remain in the chapel and pray for as long as desired: "Pray for the families. Maybe there are some of you who really want to seek the Lord yourselves and find him in a new and special way." Memories of this time in the chapel after the service portray the shared suffering:

"We all sat around in small circles, just crying or praying together. We all connected in our shared grief."[109]

"All I remember is just clinging to each other, just sobbing."[110]

"Everyone got close and grasped one another. It was quiet. There wasn't much to say. We all understood."[111]

A staff member remembered: "I remember the dead silence. Everybody sitting there in total silence."[112] A reporter from Rochester reported that when students finally left the chapel and walked into the deepening darkness, "many were holding hands."[113]

DARKNESS

Following the service, Pastor Abbott was interviewed by the *Buffalo News* and said of the students to whom he had just been ministering: "These kids aren't going to go out and get smashed because of their grief. They probably will pray together."[114] The coach of the women's volleyball team, Faithe Spurrier, invited the team over to her home for dinner "so we can keep in touch, so they have someone to be with."[115] One imagines their dinner conversation largely comprised of anecdotes about their beloved teammates, Cindy and Joy. Mary Beth Fuller recalls "just wanting to be with people who knew them. That was the overriding feeling—you just wanted to be around people who were friends of theirs." Down in the basement of East Hall, she called her parents and sobbed to them in her pain. Years later, Mary Beth's mother recalled to her how difficult it was to receive that phone call, since there was nothing parents could say to lessen the sorrow of their children.[116]

Students gathered in the lower level of the campus center to watch the late night television news in the campus snack bar. The snack bar was packed, yet silent, as the reporters described the scene and showed pictures of the twisted wreckage. The room gasped in horror as footage of a body bag being removed from the scene appeared on the screen.[117]

Cindy's roommates, Marlene Gifford and Betty Bowser, received a phone call from President Chamberlain's office that evening notifying them that Cindy's sister Debbie would like to speak with them. They went back down to campus and spoke with Debbie from the president's office for quite some time: "She just wanted to hear our voices." Upon returning to the room that the two of them had shared with Cindy, a group of friends came over to stay with them and offer some comfort. Cindy's bed was a top bunk and one of the friends unthinkingly started to climb up onto that bed. In an understandable moment of human emotion, Marlene "freaked out" at the thought of someone else being in Cindy's bed just a few hours after Cindy had—from that very spot—expressed her desire to have dinner with Marlene.[118]

October 2 was senior Kevin Danielson's twenty-first birthday. He had no specific plans for the occasion, other than a quiet evening with friends. The group of friends still gathered, but now the agenda was to watch the coverage of the accident on the TV news; there was no birthday celebration. Mark Ohl remembers the Buffalo anchorman saying words to this effect: "Although this is a terrible tragedy, students at Houghton *are taught* to think beyond this life." One of the other friends at the birthday gathering responded with frustration to that comment and said out loud to the TV: "We *believe* that; we aren't just taught it."[119]

As President Chamberlain drove to campus, he tried to firm up plans about his first steps: calling each of the students' parents and preparing for a campus memorial service. His efforts to focus on the administrative requirements of the moment were distracted, though, by his memories of The Six: "their laughter, their kindnesses, their insightful conversation, their pursuit of excellence; their faith in action had infiltrated every corner of our campus, and now the witness of their lives had suddenly turned silent. 'How can they be gone?' I said out loud, not even trying to conceal the intensity of my questions. God was the only passenger hearing my frustrations, and I kept asking more. 'How could those six have been taken? Why should any of our community be taken?'"[120]

News of the tragedy reverberated across the nation that Friday evening—to former women's volleyball coach Tanya Shire at Hope College in Michigan, to Al's former teammate Doug Roorbach at the University of Maryland, to classmate Cindy Austin who was studying for a semester at Seattle Pacific University, to former soccer player Rob Jacobsen who was working in Hawaii, and to countless others in myriad locations.

Nowhere was the news as devastating, though, as it must have been in the six homes of the six sets of parents who lost a child that Friday. Parents who had woken up that morning with the typical concerns of any normal family in the early 1980s and who, by the end of the day, had experienced the loss that is perhaps the worst pain that life can bring. In the Bushart home, in Marion, New York, all six of Al's siblings gathered to be with each other and with their bereaved parents. Everyone was in the kitchen, either sitting around the kitchen table or standing right nearby. Mrs. Bushart had the coffee pot on, as she always did. Al's younger brother Kevin remembers the scene: "It was just silent. Everyone staring straight ahead. No one said much; we shared hugs and tears. I didn't sleep much that night."[121] Similar scenes likely unfolded as wrecked families gathered and wept in the Anderson home in Danielson, Connecticut, the Andes home in Pottstown, Pennsylvania, the Ellis home in Watertown, New York, the Rapp home in Harrington Park, New Jersey, and the Rudes home in Genoa, Ohio.

October 2, 1981, came to a close with echoes of the weeping prophet:

This is what the Lord says:
"A voice is heard in Ramah,
mourning and great weeping,
Rachel weeping for her children
and refusing to be comforted,
because they are no more." (Jer. 31:15)

AFTERMATH

⸻

THE WEEKEND

If the parents of The Six slept at all Friday night, they must have awakened on Saturday morning with the hope that it was all just a horrible dream. Instead, dawn on Saturday brought with it the nightmarish realities of losing a child: identifying and claiming the lifeless body, collecting personal effects, notifying loved ones, making funeral arrangements, managing the daily necessities of life, all while dealing with one's own soul-crushing grief. One imagines members of the six families making rushed, disbelieving, tear-filled trips to Buffalo, to Houghton, and back home again, as they tended to the demands placed upon them by virtue of the previous day's horror. President Chamberlain called all of them at some point during the day "to assure them we were praying for them and concerned about them."[1]

On Saturday, Mr. and Mrs. Andes called Beth's best friend and housemate, Mercy. Beth had selected a beautiful formal dress that she would wear at her senior flute recital, perhaps one she had sewn herself, and the Andeses asked Mercy if she would retrieve that dress from Beth's closet and bring it to them at a funeral home in Buffalo. On her way to make the solemn delivery, Mercy stopped at the intersection where her friend had breathed her last. For a few moments, she quietly took in the many fingerprints of the collision: skid marks, disturbed soil, gashes in the tree. She somehow managed to complete her mission—handing Beth's parents the dress that was intended for a glorious celebration of Beth's musical accomplishments but would now be worn in her casket. Later in the day, Mercy called Beth's flute teacher and told him about the accident. When he asked if Beth was in the hospital, Mercy had to say the dreadful words: "Beth is dead."[2]

Math professor "Jake" Jacobsen and his son Steve made a Saturday morning trip to the off-campus house where Joy Ellis and Cindy Rudes both lived. Steve was friends with all six girls who lived in the house, and the night before had offered to the four who remained that he and his father would come back the next day and pack up Joy's and Cindy's belongings for them. On Joy's desk was a reminder she had left for herself to bake brownies for her younger brother Don.[3] Cindy's items were loaded into her car by her friends so that her missionary parents could easily remove it all when they visited campus.[4] At some point over the weekend, Mr. and Mrs. Rapp came to campus from New Jersey and gathered Bert's belongings.[5] Similar processes must have unfolded for all six through the weekend, as Dr. Shannon commented to a journalist on Monday that "personal effects of the victims have all been taken care of."[6]

The campus was shaken and still. A senior who walked across the campus on Saturday morning was struck by how completely quiet everything was: "No birds were chirping. No insects were buzzing around. No wind. It was eerie, as though all of creation was mourning with us."[7] A senior who was good friends with all six had been off campus on Friday, and returned to campus on Saturday to find that "the aura over the whole place was completely somber."[8] A student and his girlfriend were sitting in front of Brookside dormitory, discussing the events of the previous day, when a car drove onto the campus that was filled with students who were laughing and shouting. What would have been perfectly normal any other Saturday seemed shockingly out of place on a campus gripped by grief; it seems likely that they had not yet heard the news.[9]

As difficult as it is to believe in this age of instant information, news of the accident was still reaching people for the first time throughout the weekend. One of Bert Rapp's housemates was in Pennsylvania on Friday and Saturday and didn't get back to Houghton until Sunday evening. He saw a note that a housemate had left on the door of his room—"Call me as soon as you get in"—

and received the news shortly thereafter. The parents of this student lived in Massachusetts and had already heard in the media about an accident that had killed six Houghton students. For much of the weekend, however, they did not know the names of the students and, since their son was not on campus, were not able to contact him to ease their fears.[10] A faculty member, his wife, and their two small children were away at a religious retreat for the weekend and didn't return to their home in Houghton until Sunday. The student who lived with them didn't want them to learn the news from the headline of the Sunday newspaper that had been delivered to their front door, so he picked up the newspaper and took it to his room. When the family arrived home, he asked the parents if he could speak with them in private. Once they were alone, he gave them the news—and their newspaper.[11]

The newspapers that were arriving on the front steps in Houghton were reflective of the extensive media coverage that the accident began to receive over this first weekend. Friday evening's *Buffalo Evening News* carried the headline "Six Killed in Truck-Car Collision" with the subtitle "Victims in Wales All Young." The six were identified only as "college-age men and women," and a large photo of the twisted wreckage brought the horror of the scene to life. The headline of Saturday morning's *Buffalo Courier Express* read "6 Students Killed in Auto Collision," with a second story titled "Homecoming Plans Led to Fatal Journey." Yearbook photos of all six, which must have been provided by the college, showed their young, smiling faces. Saturday morning's headline in the *Rochester Democrat & Chronicle* stated, "6 Houghton Students Killed" with the subtitle "Wayne County man among the crash victims" (referring to Al Bushart). A map showed the location of the crash site in relation to Rochester, Buffalo, and Houghton. Similar headlines and photos appeared throughout the weekend in numerous newspapers across the state and region; even the eminent *New York Times* included a four-paragraph article on Saturday.

In his office at the Houghton Wesleyan Church, Rev. Abbott wondered how he could best minister to the grieving community in worship on Sunday morning. Specifically, what would he say in his sermon? What words would be adequate? How could he help people make sense of what had happened? As a believer in long-term sermon planning, he was in the middle of a sermon series that had been scheduled and organized months in advance. He remembers his dilemma as follows: "Would I preach what I had planned? Instead, I remember turning to the James 4:13f. passage. I have never forgotten being drawn to that passage and my own response to that Scripture about the frailty and uncertainty of human life, even the lives of vital, Christian, young adults."[12]

> *Now listen, you who say, "Today or tomorrow we will go to this or that city, spend a year there, carry on business and make money." Why, you do not even know what will happen tomorrow. What is your life? You are a mist that appears for a little while and then vanishes. Instead, you ought to say, "If it is the Lord's will, we will live and do this or that." (James 4:13–15)*

One person in the congregation on Sunday morning recalled shortly afterward that Abbott was "urging everyone to recognize how short and uncertain life is and to live in daily obedience to Christ."[13]

COLLEGE RESUMES

With the campus flag in front of Fancher Hall flying at half-staff, Professor Ruth Hutton's Oral Interpretation class met as scheduled on Monday morning. Instead of hearing Al's poetry reading, the class cried together and remembered the Scripture reading that Al had shared with his fellow students in class devotions the previous week. "I've been thinking about death a lot lately," he had said, and then read these words of Christ from John 14: "Let not your heart be troubled, you believe in God, believe also in me. In my Father's house are many mansions."[14] The complex and conflicted feelings with which Hutton's class grappled were present across the campus—a resumption of some normal activity, yet the realization that nothing was normal. An overwhelming sense of grief, but that grief tempered with faith and hope.

College administrators faced a dizzying array of urgent priorities: communication with families, caring for students, decisions about campus activities, handling the media, sending representatives to the six funerals, planning a campus memorial service, and tending to the needs of their own families. In an interview several years later, Dr. Chamberlain remembered it all as "incredibly overwhelming."[15] Bob Danner recalled everyone being "still very much in a state of shock."[16]

No changes were made to the class schedule. Danner explained, "We plan to return to the normalcy of collegiate life, if that is possible after the loss of six very important people."[17] In classes where one of the accident victims had been a student, faculty members were advised to use their own discretion about holding class.[18] Attendance in classes was light, however, as students were traveling to memorial services or were presumably too distraught to focus on academics.[19]

What to do about homecoming? How could the campus celebrate in the wake of such a tragedy and without the senior members of the homecoming court? The homecoming committee met with President Chamberlain on Monday morning to discuss alternatives. Although the possibility of cancelling homecoming was discussed, students and administrators agreed to press ahead with one major modification to the schedule: there would be no coronation of a homecoming queen. Key factors in the decision to proceed with homecoming included the logistics of notifying on short notice the many alumni who had already made plans to attend, the desire to honor the six students at homecoming, and the belief that The Six would want the traditions of homecoming to continue.[20] Senior class president Allen Hemayakian commented, "We haven't made definite plans about how to handle all this yet, but we know it won't be the same."[21]

Almost everyone on the small, tightly knit, residential campus knew at least one of The Six—from having the same classes, living in the same residence hall, playing on the same athletic team, participating in the same musical ensemble or club, or eating in the same dining hall. "They were like family," one classmate remembered. "At Houghton, we were all family."[22] Even most freshmen, who were only five weeks into their college experience and minimally integrated into the student body, were probably familiar with Alan Bushart from his exploits on the soccer field that fall. If students didn't know one of The Six personally, they probably knew someone who did. The deaths weren't abstract and distant; they were up close and personal. A faculty member remembers how "somber" the campus was in those first days.[23] A journalist wrote of "the pall that has hung over the hilltop campus since the accident in Wales Center."[24]

The responsibility of caring for the grieving student body fell primarily to the Dean of Students Office. Danner recalls that the students who needed the most support were those who were close friends of The Six and those who were angry at God for the tragedy. But even students who weren't impacted in those ways had numerous questions and struggles: "What does all this mean? How do I fit into all that's happening? How do I help my friends? Is it even okay to try to study?" The demands for counseling were heavy, and the director of Houghton's counseling center had resigned a month before the accident. Short-staffed, Danner tapped members of the church staff, the religion faculty, and the Student Life staff to step in and offer direct support to students. "We were on task and numb," he recalls, "trying to think of all the things that we needed to do for the benefit of the students, the families, and the college. We did the best we could."[25]

Houghton's director of public information, Dean Liddick, had been away at a family reunion in Philadelphia throughout the weekend and did not learn of the accident until he returned to Houghton late Sunday night. Liddick went to his office early Monday morning and began responding to the "flood" of requests from the media for information, while possessing only limited information himself. A Christian radio station interviewed him live on Monday and he recalls: "I barely got through it. I was creating lots of dead air space for them. I couldn't keep going. The emotion of it all was too much."[26]

Members of the media descended upon the campus. In their interviews with students, journalists discovered young men and women who were shattered by the tragedy, but also tenaciously holding on to deep faith in these first days of grief. Susan Facer, Student Senate president, said to a reporter: "We believe they are in heaven. And we believe we'll be united with them someday. I don't want to say we don't ask 'Why?' because we do. Ultimately, we have a peace about them. We miss them, but we know it's temporary."[27] Gil Morgan, who shared an apartment with Al Bushart said: "It's comforting to know they're in a better place than us."[28] Elizabeth White, a junior, remarked: "Sure, we are grieving because we miss our friends, but we are rejoicing at the same time. We're confident we will see them again."[29]

Rich Newburg, a television reporter from Channel 4 in Buffalo, flew to campus on Tuesday. Students were astonished to see the station's helicopter land on the athletic field, and Mr. Newburg then spent a couple hours on campus conducting interviews and filming. Near the end of his visit, he spoke with President Chamberlain and a group of student leaders on the portico in front of Wesley Chapel. Mary Beth Fuller, junior class chaplain, said of her close friend Joy Ellis, "She's the happiest now she's ever been. She's with the Lord, and that's the ultimate homecoming."[30] Viewing the students' deaths in this light—as a sort of homecoming—would become an oft-repeated and iconic theme of the days to come. The station helicopter lifted off shortly thereafter, carrying Mr. Newburg and the crew to the Rochester area for the funeral of one of The Six.

SIX FUNERALS

Funeral arrangements for the six students were printed on a half-sheet of paper and distributed at the Houghton Wesleyan Church on Sunday and across the campus on Monday.[31] With the names of the students listed in alphabetical order, the campus community was provided with basic information about funeral homes, churches, and service times. The Student Senate assisted in coordinating rides, and caravans of cars departed the campus throughout the week for the various services. Some students, especially seniors, attended multiple services. At least one administrative or faculty representative of the college also attended each service, with the first funeral (Mark Anderson's) taking place on Monday, October 4, and the final one (Bert Rapp's) on Saturday, October 10.

The memorial service for Mark Anderson took place at the Tillinghast Funeral Home in Danielson, Connecticut, on Monday at 11:00 a.m. Mark's brother Keith, the medical resident, had asked to see Mark's body but was advised not to do so. Approximately two hundred people attended the service, including sizable contingents from the Andersons' former church and from Houghton. One of Mark's brothers recalls, "My mom was severely broken up, and Dad was the strong one, but over time that reversed itself."[32] Another brother commented, "Houghton really showed up at the funeral. The strong presence of Houghton people was sustaining in that moment. It was clear that he was loved and respected and cared for, and that's how you want your son or brother to be seen."[33]

The memorial service for Joy Ellis was held at Parkside Bible Church in Watertown, New York, also on Monday at 11:00 a.m. Joy's father was the pastor of the church, but it is not known if he officiated or spoke at the service. Joy had recently mentioned to her mother that, when she died, she wanted an "open house" that would allow her friends and family members to get acquainted with one another, and then everyone could go together to the memorial service afterward.[34] Joy's Houghton friends who attended the service remember a gathering with lots of food at the Ellis home, so Joy's request was apparently honored.[35]

Beth Andes' funeral occurred at the Williams Funeral Home in Skippack, Pennsylvania, on Tuesday at 1:00 p.m. It was one of the largest funeral services that the funeral home had ever hosted.[36] Beth's close friend Mercy remembers a vigorous debate among some of Beth's friends about the wisdom of traveling to the service; the understandable concern was that they were so distraught and exhausted that they might also get into a car accident. After consulting with parents, the group of four friends did make the trip. Mercy met Beth's two sisters, parents, and other family members and "just loved them." On the long ride back to Houghton, Mercy caught herself thinking that upon her return to campus she would walk into the room next to hers and tell Beth how much she enjoyed meeting her family. Instead, she had to walk by the door of Beth's empty room for the rest of the semester and absorb the stillness and loss.[37]

Second Reformed Church in Marion, New York, just east of Rochester, was the site of the memorial service for Alan Bushart on Tuesday at 2:00 p.m. Approximately 500 people packed into the church, including large numbers of Houghton students who were able to make the relatively short drive. The helicopter carrying Rich Newburg from Channel 4 landed at the nearby fire hall. Coach Burke brought words of condolence on behalf of the college. In the funeral sermon, Alan's pastor talked about how Alan's life embodied the biblical words of the apostle Paul: "I have fought the good fight, I have finished the race, I have kept the faith" (2 Timothy 4:7). The service closed with the congregation singing "Because He Lives"—a gospel song and Bushart family favorite about the hope of Christ's resurrection.[38] An attendee recalls how shattered Mrs. Bushart looked during the service but as this closing song started, she turned to the family members surrounding her and said, "Let's sing it like we mean it."[39] She must have been a tower of strength, for a few minutes later, when she was standing at her son's graveside and the sun peeked out from behind the clouds for a moment, she turned to her son Kevin and said, "Son Touched"—a reference to the musical ministry team in which Al sang at Houghton.[40]

Cindy Rudes' funeral took place at the Robinson Funeral in Genoa, Ohio, near Toledo, also on Tuesday afternoon. Her sister Debbie had arrived in Genoa over the weekend and driven to a nearby mall to pick out a dress for Cindy to be buried in; to the Detroit airport to pick up their grieving and exhausted parents who had just arrived from Hong Kong after twenty-five hours of travel; and then back to Genoa. She remembers the family meeting at the funeral home to pick out the casket: "My parents were just devastated. We were trying to pick out a casket and no one could say anything or decide anything. Finally, my boyfriend Dan (now my husband) said simply: 'I think Cindy would like this one. It's wood, warmer than metal.' Dad said, 'okay,' and that was it."[41] The casket was open at the service, and friends remember the shock of seeing her dead body; one remembers the red fingernail polish on her folded hands.[42] The service included the singing of the hymn "Great Is Thy Faithfulness," words of tribute to Cindy, the reading of a letter of condolence from Houghton College, words of encouragement from the pastor who twenty-one years earlier had performed Cindy's baby dedication, and the singing of Cindy's favorite worship chorus: "Praise the Lord, praise the Lord, let the earth hear his voice." Following the service, members of the women's volleyball team presented the Rudes with a Houghton blanket.[43] A classmate of Cindy's who went to the funeral spoke briefly with Mr. Rudes in the receiving line; he referenced the words of the calamity-stricken Job: "The Lord gives, and the Lord takes away."[44]

Bert Rapp's family held a private service for family members the day after the accident; a public memorial service was held at Harrington Park Community Church in New Jersey on Saturday, October 10, at 3:00 p.m. Dr. David Frazier, a faculty member in the business department, was the college representative at Bert's service and was asked to say a few words on behalf of the college. Frazier was close to Bert and got choked up as he remembered the moment: "It was unquestionably the most emotional and stressful experience I have ever had. I have never done anything that difficult. My heart was beating so hard, I thought I was going to have a heart attack. The emotion of what the family was going through, that has always stuck with me. The loss of my own parents, the loss of one of my own sisters—nothing was as traumatic and emotional as Bert's funeral."[45] Bert's girlfriend, Karyn, shared with the congregation a reflection from C. S. Lewis' The Chronicles of Narnia, during which she read the final words of the final book in the series: "All their life in this world and all their adventures in Narnia had only been the cover and the title page; now at last they were beginning Chapter One of the Great Story, which no one on earth has read; which goes on forever; in which every chapter is better than the one before."[46] One of Bert's housemates and close friends recalls: "All I remember about Bert's funeral was not wanting it to be true."[47]

But it was true. Six leaders. Six friends. Six sons and daughters. Six funerals. A student who attended three of the funerals remembers: "Those first few days were constant reminders—they're all gone. They're just gone. I remember lots of tears, feeling the utter shock of it all. I think we were all in shock. There was so much excitement about their senior year, but it all changed. They were gone. It was so hard."[48]

CAMPUS MEMORIAL SERVICE

Cards, letters, and telegrams from around the country began to pour into the campus. Large bulletin boards in the campus center lounge displayed them, under a sign that read "Expressions of Sympathy and Support."[49] Within just a few feet of the spot where the six students met for their trip to Buffalo, students now stood and read messages of condolence about their deaths:[50]

> Each of us here at St. Bonaventure University have been deeply saddened by the tragic, untimely deaths of the six young students from Houghton College. I wish to express my own personal sorrow along with that of our entire university community. Please be assured of remembrance in our prayers—especially the prayers of our students—for the families of the deceased, the students, and the Houghton College community. We pray that God's comforting grace will be with all of you.
>
> —Mathias Doyle, President

> The senior class at Roberts Wesleyan College would like you to know in a special way that we care, and are sharing your feelings of deep hurt, shock, and loss at this time. The news of the loss of your six classmates and friends hit very hard here also—being seniors at a small Christian college where everybody knows everybody. . . . We as a class have been praying for you.
>
> Our prayers are with you as we share in your sorrow. Now may the Lord of peace himself give you peace in all times and all ways.
>
> —The students of Bethel College

Nearly two hundred of these messages arrived on campus, from a wide variety of colleges and universities, churches, alumni, and friends of the college. A sympathy card was even signed by the nine members of the seventh-grade class at St. Thomas More Church in Rochester. This "outpouring of love and comfort" brought a measure of strength to the grieving campus.[51]

Even as the campus was receiving this support from others, students felt compelled to extend their support to someone outside the campus community who was grieving. Dean of students, Robert Danner, reported: "I saw in our student body a compassion in another direction that seemed unusual to me at the time; there was a huge uprising of thought about the truck driver who had hit the students."[52] Similarly, Charles Massey recalls that "the students at Houghton College, in the midst of their own grieving, realized what an incredible burden the truck driver must be dealing with."[53] Students wanted Mr. Bingenheimer to know that they were concerned about his well-being and did not in any way hold him responsible for the deaths of their friends. As Rick Dibble, senior class chaplain, said to a reporter, "There is no malice here."[54]

Members of the senior class prepared a letter for Mr. Bingenheimer, which was signed by hundreds of students. On Tuesday or Wednesday, Dr. Charles Massey from the Buffalo campus was asked to deliver the letter to Mr. Bingenheimer at his home south of Buffalo. Massey remembers that the Bingenheimer family was so overwhelmed by the enormity of the tragedy that they were not eager to see anyone from the college. Mr. Bingenheimer did agree, however, to the personal delivery of a letter. "He met with me just long enough that I could express the concern of the community for him. I gave the letter to him and had a brief prayer and left. He was appreciative—moved—but it was quick. He was dealing with this tragedy in a way none of us can imagine."[55] At the campus memorial service on Wednesday evening, President Chamberlain made these comments about Mr. Bingenheimer's receipt of the letter: "He was deeply moved by the reaction of parents and students, and he has requested me to share his great appreciation for the prayers and kind expressions of concern for him. He further extends his condolences to the families and friends of these students."[56] Massey was not aware of any subsequent visits between anyone from the college and Mr. Bingenheimer. "Any further contact was just going to be a reminder of the worst day of his life."[57]

On Wednesday evening at 7:00 p.m., the Houghton community gathered in Wesley Chapel for the memorial service that President Chamberlain began planning shortly after he heard the stunning news. The 1200-seat auditorium was filled to overflowing, with folding chairs set up in the lobby to accommo-date the crowd of approximately 1350.[58] In addition to current faculty, staff, administrators, and students, the congregation included recent graduates, former employees, community members, trustees, and family members and friends of The Six. Most notably, the parents of five of the six victims were in attendance—most of whom had stood at the graveside of their son or daughter within the last couple days. Only the parents of Beth Andes were unable to attend.[59] Many members of the media were also present, with clear instructions from the college that they were to be unobtrusive and discreet.[60]

The simple half-sheet printed program was entitled, "Service of Worship to the Glory of God and in Memory of Mark Anderson, Beth Andes, Alan Bushart, Joy Ellis, Albert Rapp and Cynthia Rudes." A note at the bottom asked attendees to refrain from flash photography and informed the congregation that those serving as ushers were representatives of the Young Administrators Organization, the men's soccer team, the women's volleyball team, and the wind ensemble—organizations to which at least one of The Six had belonged.[61] As the hushed congregation listened to the organ prelude of "A Mighty Fortress Is Our God" and J. S. Bach's arrangement of "Jesus, Priceless Treasure," many were "clutching handkerchiefs."[62]

Pastor Mark Abbott welcomed the congregation with these words: "We welcome you not primarily to a service of sorrow, though we do experience that. Not merely to a service of memory, but certainly there is that. But rather to a service of worship and hope."[63] Abbott read briefly from 1 Thessalonians 4, where the apostle Paul reminded believers of eternal life through the resurrection of Christ and encouraged them not to "grieve like those who have no hope" (4:13), and then offered this opening prayer: "Oh God our Father, your love is stronger than death. Your power is stronger than all evil. And thus this evening, we want to hear your promises and believe them and receive the comfort they offer to us. You are the giver of hope. fill us with joy and peace in believing, so that we may have abundant hope through the power of the Holy Spirit. Through Christ we pray, Amen."

The opening hymn was "Children of the Heavenly Father"—a Swedish hymn rooted in tragic loss. The author, Karolina Sandell, witnessed the death of her father by drowning when she was twenty-six. Members of the senior class, classmates of The Six, were invited to sing the first verse alone: "Children of the heavenly Father, safely in His bosom gather / Nestling bird nor star in Heaven, such a refuge e'er was given." The entire congregation joined the seniors for the remaining verses, with these lyrics among those they tearfully sang: "Neither life nor death shall ever, from the Lord His children sever / Unto them His grace He showeth, and their sorrows all He knoweth."[64]

Four Scripture readings followed, read by representatives of the college community. Rick Dibble, senior class chaplain, read Psalm 46, which includes the statement: "God is our refuge and strength, an ever-present help in trouble." Susan Facer, president of the Student Senate, read John 14:1–6, including: "Do not let your hearts be troubled. Trust in God, trust also in me. My Father's house has plenty of room." Professor Richard Smiley, senior class advisor, read from 1 Corinthians 15, which asks the question: "Where, O death, is your victory? Where, O death, is your sting?" Finally, Pastor Mark Abbott led the congregation in a responsive reading of selected verses from Revelation 21, including: "God will wipe every tear from their eyes. There will be no more death or mourning or crying or pain, for the old order of things has passed away."

The Houghton College Choir, the premier vocal ensemble on campus, then walked quietly onto risers on the stage, dressed in black. Without two of their former members, Alan Bushart and Bert Rapp, the choir performed two numbers with their typical artistic excellence and passion. The first, "Brother James' Air," is a setting of Psalm 23: "The Lord's my Shepherd, I'll not want; / He makes me down to lie. / In pastures green, He leadeth me; / the quiet waters by. . . . Yea, though I pass through shadows death, / yet will I fear no ill; / For Thou art with me, and Thy rod / and staff me comfort still."[65] The choir then sang Isaac Watts' majestic hymn of hope and confidence: "O God, Our Help in Ages Past," which closes with these words: "O God, our Help in ages past, / our Hope for years to come, / be Thou our Guard while life shall last, / and our eternal Home."[66] One senior who was present that night remembers the men in the choir singing that last verse loudly and strongly—in tribute to the two men, Bert and Al, whose voices were absent.[67]

President Chamberlain then approached the pulpit for his address to the grieving community he led. What can you possibly say? How do you both acknowledge the unspeakable loss and simultaneously provide hope? How do you craft words so they have the compassion and elegance the situation requires? He must have labored over this message, perhaps in the early morning or late-night hours, as he also grappled with the multiple demands placed upon him over the preceding five days. "The events of last Friday shocked and saddened us all," he began. "The sudden snatching of six senior students from our community has produced tears, the pain of separation and prayers for the bereaved." He expressed gratitude for the support expressed in the many cards and letters the college had received, admiration for the "strength and courage" of the parents, and appreciation for the community's concern for the driver of the truck.

Dr. Chamberlain then gave brief words of tribute about each of the six students. These tributes became the college's official statements about The Six that would be used in a variety of contexts:

MARK ANDERSON

Mark was loved at Houghton for his warmth, for his honesty and for that particular light in his eyes that injected an air of sincere friendship into even the most acute academic discussion. Mark brought his keen mind to bear, with great success, on his pre-law history studies at Houghton, and also on the work of the Houghton College Student Development Council on which he was elected to serve this year. Everyone who worked with Mark recognized that his willingness to question and challenge was always tempered by an unquestioned faith, solidly grounded in Jesus Christ.

BETH ANDES

There was something unaffected, something disarmingly genuine about Beth that touched everyone she came in contact with during her years at Houghton. Genuinely concerned for the spiritual lives of others, she was always ready to pray with others for their needs. Loyal as a friend, she was unwilling to hold a grudge against anyone. Beth's spiritual integrity set the tone for all of her tasks. She gave herself energetically to the disciplines of an applied flute major. She participated actively in performance groups. In all of it, Beth retained her ability to laugh. And she retained always her desire to use all her talents in Christ's service.

AL BUSHART

To those he touched at Houghton, Al was both a challenge and a comfort. He set a spiritually challenging example of a strong man of God striving for excellence in all he did. As co-captain of the college soccer team, he brought energy, enthusiasm, and tremendous athletic skill. To his coursework in communications and music, he brought talent and energy of equal caliber. With his desire to touch others for God, he inspired fellow students in the college choir and in Houghton's "Son Touched" music ministry. But Al went beyond challenging others. He loved them. No one who spent any time with Al remained unmoved by his gentle and tender spirit, by his kind words, by the warmth of his attitude. He was always ready to talk about the Lord and to encourage others. Yet he never put on airs. He never employed subtlety. He never played games. He lived his life as an open book. All who have read from that book have been immeasurably enriched.

JOY ELLIS

Joy was loved at Houghton for her warmth, for her kindness, and for the solid spiritual maturity that carried over into everything she did. This maturity was reflected in the conscientious attitude she brought to her coursework in business administration and to her service in the Houghton College Student Senate. It was reflected also in the spiritual leadership she provided as chaplain of the college women's volleyball team. Sharing a poem at practice or encouraging her teammates seemed to be simply second nature with Joy. Those who knew Joy during her college years will always remember her in this way: although she was active and successful in both athletics and in her academic work, Joy always maintained the lovely, ladylike attitude of a young woman whose heart belonged to Jesus Christ.

ALBERT RAPP

During his college years, Bert gained a maturity that earned the respect and appreciation of everyone who knew him. He demonstrated this maturity by the responsible way in which he carried out his duties on the Houghton Financial Affairs Council, a college governing council that he was chosen to serve on this year. As president of the Young Administrators Organization, Bert displayed his talent as a leader of others—talent enhanced by a certain tact and kindness that always took into account the feelings of others. Most importantly, Bert had a deep-rooted faith in Jesus Christ. And he made this faith tangible. He cared about others. He was always willing to stop and listen to someone else's problems despite his own busy schedule. Few ever walked away from a conversation with Bert without having been touched by his openness, and without feeling the contagious enthusiasm and love for life that he shared so freely with others.

CYNTHIA RUDES

During her college years, Cindy was known and loved for her willingness to share of herself. Those who knew her speak of the Christ-centered joy that enabled her to take difficulties in stride. They speak of her readiness to encourage others and to offer help even when loaded down with responsibilities of her own. They remember the prayer meetings she led as senior class chaplain, and the spiritual leadership she provided as captain of the college women's volleyball team. In the same way that she was committed to serving, Cindy was also committed to learning. This was reflected in the quality of her coursework in communications and Bible. Most importantly, even while she maintained a conscientious attitude toward studies, she always considered her academic achievements to be valuable only insofar as they trained her to be a more effective servant of Jesus Christ.

Chamberlain shared a couple personal anecdotes that illustrated the generosity and kindness of the six students, and noted that due to their humility, most had not even told their parents that they were members of the homecoming court. He then reflected on a chapel talk he had given to the student body just the week before: "I suggested four principles growing out of the life and experience of Joseph. They were these: maintain a concern for others; recognize God's blessing even in adversity; remain tender; exhibit a spirit of forgiveness. These young people were living examples of these four principles. Their lives strengthened us and their memories will enrich us."

Dr. Chamberlain then drew the congregation's attention to two passages of Scripture from the New Testament. From the account in John's gospel of Jesus weeping at the death of his friend Lazarus, Dr. Chamberlain pointed out two "fundamental truths": the reality of eternal life and the assurance that Lazarus' death "had been permitted by God to bring glory to God." Consequently, Chamberlain said, "That is our confidence. God is in control, and he will bring honor and glory to himself. Christ is the resurrection and the life and because he lives, we too shall live." Drawing a contrast with those who would suggest that life has no meaning, he said: "The purpose of life is to glorify God. History is not circular nor meaningless; it is linear. It proceeds from God and it is his desire that life lead us to him."

Drawing on Luke's account of the two disheartened disciples traveling to Emmaus after the crucifixion, Chamberlain said: "Yes, for them Friday was a dark day, but Sunday was coming. We have had our dark Friday, but Sunday is coming. The separation we experienced on Friday is temporary; Sunday is coming." His voice breaking with emotion as he said the students' names one more time, Dr. Chamberlain concluded his message: "And so to Mark, Beth, Alan, Joy, Bert, and Cindy we do not say 'goodbye.' We say, 'Till we meet again.'"

The eleven-member musical ensemble Son Touched, in which Al had participated, performed two numbers: "The Highest Praise" and "No One Ever Cared for Me like Jesus." Pastor Abbott offered a prayer of thanksgiving and hope: "For the witness they left to a watching world, even through their death, how we praise you. For the memories which are sad but sweet, we thank you. For the challenge of their lives and their death, the challenge to be more fully yours, the challenge to be more effective instruments of your peace, we praise you. And even for the questions stimulated by the tragedy, which cause us to examine afresh the meaning of life and death, we thank you." Abbott's prayer closed by asking God to comfort parents and family members, the truck driver, and the entire community. The congregation then prayed the Lord's Prayer in unison.

The one-hour service closed with the congregation joining together to sing "Oh, the Deep, Deep Love of Jesus." With the rich tones of the immense Holtkamp pipe organ resounding through the chapel, these words washed over the grieving community: "O the deep, deep love of Jesus, / vast, unmeasured, boundless, free, / rolling as a mighty ocean / in its fullness over me. / Underneath me, all around me, / is the current of Thy love; / leading onward, leading homeward, / to Thy glorious rest above."[68]

In their reporting about the service, the *Olean Times Herald* noted that "Houghton College mourns, not as an institution with 1200 students, but as a family" and that "throughout the service, students, for the most part, seemed almost serene, sitting quietly with bowed heads."[69] One attendee remembers Dr. Chamberlain's message as "magnificent."[70] Cindy Rudes' parents described the service as "a time of comfort and healing."[71] A member of the class of 1981 who had borrowed a car to drive from Maryland for the memorial service reflected on the gathering: "I remember feeling the Comforter at work."[72] A number of students remained in the slowly emptying chapel for some time afterward, "clustered together, crying, and comforting each other."[73]

Parents and other family members of The Six were invited to a private reception after the service. College representatives escorted the families to a room on campus, told the families that this was an informal gathering with no program, and then left the families alone to meet and comfort one another. "The college was very sensitive about how horrific this was for all of us," a sibling of one of The Six reported.[74] Although their children had been in a serious dating relationship for many months, the families of Cindy Rudes and Al Bushart had never met. The two fathers, upon meeting, "shook hands, smiled, and one said to the other, 'I guess you and I would have been in-laws.'"[75] The two broken-hearted fathers hugged each other and wept.

While the families were meeting with one another, President Chamberlain and Susan Facer, president of the Student Senate, met with members of the press in a college lecture hall. Dr. Chamberlain reported that the college would be establishing a presidential scholarship in memory of the six students. Chamberlain was asked if he was satisfied with the conclusion of the police that the accident was caused by the failure of the students' car to stop at the intersection. Chamberlain responded: "I've been at the intersection many, many times, and the first few times, it came at me suddenly." He commented that a student who was unfamiliar with that road could easily miss the stop sign, particularly in a carload of six "happily engaged in conversation." He also pointed out that the roadway was wet.[76] Chamberlain was asked what Houghton's message to the world is through this tragedy. He responded: "Our message is that faith works all the time. . . . We are tested in faith during times of great tragedy, and although we do not understand everything, faith gives us the assurance that God rules."[77]

Susan Facer reported that although the deaths have left a great void on campus, she "felt a unity" in the student body since the accident, and that "the students have really pulled together and supported each other." Speaking of the grief of the student body, she said: "Of course any death brings sorrow, but their deaths are not without hope." Each of The Six, she reported, "had Jesus Christ as his Savior personally."[78] Chamberlain reported that the student body supported the college's decision to proceed with homecoming, and Facer agreed: "Because, in a sense, our six friends are in the home of the Lord."[79]

INTERSECTION OUTCRY

The community in which the accident occurred, the Town of Wales, and surrounding communities were also feeling the aftershocks of the worst accident in the region's history. Stunned residents and community leaders erupted with an immediate outcry for changes to the hazardous intersection. On Tuesday, the same day that three of the six students were being buried, local county and state officials met in the Town of Wales town hall to determine how the intersection (and one other deemed dangerous) could be made safer. Erie County legislator William Paxon remarked that the meeting's purpose was to "speed up actions needed to get these intersections signalized or marked."[80] Paxon suggested a five-point plan: lower the speed limit; install a flasher; set up better "stop ahead" signs on Route 78; increase police patrols; and rebuild the intersection so that motorists approaching from the south do so at a 90-degree angle rather than the current gentle curve.[81] The *Buffalo Evening News* reported on October 7 that the accident "may bring speedier-than-usual remedial action from the State Department of Transportation."[82]

The local community newspaper, *The East Aurora Advertiser,* printed several letters to the editor that expressed concern about the intersection and frustration that steps had not already been taken to remediate those concerns. A letter signed by Robert L. Kowalewski stated: "It is tragically regrettable that we have been unable to cope with the catastrophic problems we face on Routes 20A and 78 in our Town of Wales. As a substantial property owner fronting right on 20A, my family and our neighbors have been and are continually terrified by this situation. Any further delay of realistic action by responsible authorities can only smack of flagrant disregard for human life."[83] A letter written on behalf of the board of directors of the Wales Business Association suggested flashing lights, a speed limit reduction, and a redesign of the entire intersection. The letter concluded with this passionate plea: "Let us stop the rhetoric and cut through the red tape to improve the traffic control at this HAZARDOUS INTERSECTION."[84]

A letter written on October 5 by a local resident to the Erie County Sheriff's Office said: "People aren't running that stop sign on 78 and 20A, they're pulling out for the left turn before it's safe because their view to the right is blocked. . . . A driver may be so disturbed and preoccupied trying to look to the right that he might not give enough attention to the left also. The left-turn approach to the stop sign has to be made more perpendicular to 20A."[85] An anonymous letter to the editor poetically portrays the community's sorrow:

A sheriff's car screams past, and then another. In the distance more sirens wail—the flow of traffic on busy 20A past the house stops, and my heart stops. Another bad one—who is it? Who in the community are we going to be mourning with—is it one of our own? It is not one of our own—it is six young people from a college out of town, but we mourn anyway. The horror of it fills the community. . . . What more will it take to get the signal? The eye-catching warning traffic light that will alert out-of-town drivers and all the rest of us that this is a dangerous intersection, that 78 is coming onto heavily-traveled 20A and not just meandering serenely around yet another gentle curve.

Called "Too Late," the letter ends with the hope that action taken won't be too late to save the life of the author's young daughter.[86]

HOMECOMING

On Thursday morning, which would have been Joy Ellis' twenty-first birthday, the flag on campus was restored to full staff and attention turned to preparations for homecoming weekend. "Our sorrow needs to end," said Dr. Chamberlain.[87] I do not think Dr. Chamberlain or anyone believed that the community's grief was anywhere near complete, but rather hoped that campus life could now begin to resume a greater degree of normalcy. In the campus center lounge, near the display of telegrams and letters of condolence, posters appeared that said: "Wear your hats and bring your shakers to the game this Saturday! Show your spirit for Homecoming!"[88] Days after being floored by unimaginable loss, the campus would now attempt to get up and host a celebration.

Homecoming activities would proceed largely as planned. Tours of the recently completed (and still unnamed) physical education center next to Shenawana would be conducted. An exhibit of paintings and sculptures by the Houghton art faculty was on display in the Wesley Chapel gallery. The annual contests between alumni and the volleyball, field hockey, and junior varsity soccer teams would take place on the athletic fields on Saturday. Dr. Shannon commented that homecoming would be "as normal as possible."[89]

The festivities officially began with the traditional Founder's Day chapel on Friday morning. Faculty processed into Wesley Chapel in their academic regalia, led by senior faculty member Dr. George Wells. In his opening remarks, Dr. Chamberlain connected the accident to the college's mission: "As a Christian liberal arts college, our goal is to provide spiritual and intellectual nurture. It is our purpose to prepare our students for two commencements. The usual first marks the conclusion of an undergraduate program and the beginning of a career, the beginning of a profession, the beginning of graduate school. That second and more important commencement is the beginning of eternal life. This year, as I'm sure all of you know, that usual order was reversed for six of our seniors. They had that second commencement without the first. And we now know that they are in the nearer presence of our Lord, and we rejoice in that certain knowledge. We also seek to receive and share God's comfort with their families and friends who are here with us."[90] The keynote address was delivered by Rev. Dr. Lee Haines, general secretary of education and the ministry for The

Wesleyan Church. Honorary doctoral degrees were presented to Dr. Haines and to Houghton alumnus Dr. Wilfred Bain, former member of the music faculty and founder of the college choir.

The student newspaper, the *Houghton Star,* released its weekly issue on Friday afternoon. Instead of the typical articles about college events and letters to the editor that opined about campus and contemporary issues, the October 9, 1981, issue was fully dedicated to the lives and memories of the six seniors who had been killed seven days before. The front-page headline was a quotation of Christ's words in John 11: "I am the resurrection and the life; he that believeth in me, though he were dead, yet shall he live: and whosoever liveth and believeth in me shall never die" (John 11:25–26 KJV). Immediately below, centered inside a decorative border, appeared the bolded words "In Memory of" with the six students' names listed beneath.[91]

The issue did not feature in-depth reporting about the accident, the memorial service, or any other dimension of the campus response. Instead, the issue was comprised simply and beautifully of words of remembrance about each of the six students, written by their fellow students and other members of the campus community. Sprinkled among these tributes were Scripture quotations, expressions of support that had been sent to the campus, quotes from authors such as C. S. Lewis and John Donne, and photographs of The Six. Co-editors Linda Ippolito and Glenn Burlingame included this brief explanatory note about the issue's purpose: "It is our hope that this Issue of the *Star* will help you to hold close memories of those whose lives we shared and loved, and also to remember that they are now with their Father."[92]

These words of tribute provide a contemporaneous glimpse into the genuine affection students had for their departed friends. One brief excerpt from the *Star's* tributes for each of The Six follows:[93]

FOR MARK ANDERSON:

I remember walking with Mark to the end of a jetty in the Ketchikan, Alaska, harbor and discussing at length what it means to be a Christian and how a Christian is to act—all the while enjoying an Alaskan sunset. Mark's gregariousness was balanced by a love of solitude, his quick wit by a far-reaching sensitivity; his love of argumentation by a deep concern for fairness. Mark's life wasn't as symmetrical as this essay. Mark was human—asymmetrical, imperfect. What made Mark an exceptional person was his candid recognition of his humanness. —Glenn Burlingame

FOR BETH ANDES:

It is said that one finds only a few true friends in the course of a lifetime. For me, Beth Renee Andes was the truest friend I could ever desire. Her honesty and sincerity was never doubted for she was certainly that 'friend who sticks closer than a brother' (Proverbs 18:24). She was always ready to listen, and especially to pray as we shared our concerns, whether they were confusions about personal relationships, or whether it was supporting each other through flute recitals. —Mercy Zecher

FOR ALAN BUSHART:

Al was an excellent co-captain of our soccer team, in that though he provided the disciplined example of a strong leading athlete, he related to each of his teammates a sincere Christian love. Though Al loved to push us to our limit physically, he was always there to encourage those of us that were especially struggling. Al had a sincere desire to glorify God through his soccer and strove to instill that same goal in all of our hearts. Al loved the game, deeply appreciated the support of the spectators and most of all loved the Father who allowed him to play. —Tim Edwards

FOR JOY ELLIS:

For my dearly loved friend Joy Suzanne, a song by Amy Grant, because she always wanted it to be true of her, and because it is. "She had her Father's eyes. Her Father's eyes—Eyes that found the good in things, when help could not be found. Eyes full of compassion, feeling every pain. Knowing what you're going through, and feeling it the same. Just like her Father's eyes." —Chris Davidson

FOR BERT RAPP:

To remember Bert Rapp is to remember what he believed in: quietly but forcefully change the injustices of society. With a quick wit, a smile and intelligent, well-thought-out words, Bert worked behind the scenes as his father had taught him: to accept what could not be changed but try within the system to correct what could be corrected. Bert was always a gentleman, ambitious, hardworking, and always willing to do a favor or to help. —Austin Swallow

FOR CINDY RUDES:

Cindy meant so much to all who knew her. Some words might be witty, funny, caring—so caring, loving—full of life and love of life. God was the key to her. Her relationship with Christ meant everything. Christ was someone she lived with personally every day and shared with anyone who would listen. She was always so ready to share what God had been doing for her. He always provided for her needs and she assured us he would do the same for us. She will be missed. What an understatement! But we loved her as our sister and will feel her loss for a long time. —Betty Bowser

A collage of candid photos of The Six filled the back page: smiling with friends, playing their sport, practicing their instrument, sleeping on their books in the library.

The campus center dining hall was decorated with a Wild West theme for dinner on Friday evening. A production of the opera *Lucia di Lammermoor* was staged by the Eastern Opera Theatre of New York at 8:00 p.m. in Wesley Chapel.[94] At 11:00 p.m., students and alumni climbed to the top of the ski slope and ate donuts and drank hot chocolate around a large, crackling bonfire. One student commented to a reporter who was present: "We really don't have anything to be gloomy about. Those who died had their own homecoming . . . they've gone home now."[95]

The campus was sun-drenched on Saturday, which must have provided a modest lift to the mood on campus. The road that encircled the campus was the route of the Wild West float parade which began at 10:00 a.m. Each class had managed to design and build a Western-themed float in the preceding days of grief, and now they showed their handiwork to the rest of campus. Riding on or near the floats of the freshman, sophomore, and junior classes were the women who had been selected by each class as the homecoming court and the men who were their escorts. Yearbook photos show floats portraying a stagecoach, a Western saloon, and a Native American village. President and Mrs. Chamberlain, dressed in pioneer attire, rode together perched on the back of a classic convertible. Clowns in cowboy garb, happy cheerleaders on a hay-wagon, horses and carriages, and the Highlander bagpiper rounded out the parade line-up. From the smiles on the faces of the parade participants and the spectators standing alongside the parade route, many of them also decked out in Western gear, one gets the impression of a perfectly normal and utterly joyful Houghton homecoming parade on a clear, crisp autumn day.[96]

The highlight of the parade, though, was to have been the three senior homecoming queen candidates and their escorts riding in horse-drawn carriages, followed by the senior class float. But there were no queen candidates. No escorts. And the senior class float portrayed a small, simple Western church—utterly silent and empty. The float had somehow been built by the seniors that week. The co-chair of homecoming commented, "It's unbelievable how the whole class pitched in, when everyone could have just gone to pieces."[97] The senior class named their float "Through It All"—the song the campus had sung together at the initial campus meeting in Wesley Chapel the night of the accident. A member of the junior class who was in the parade recalls, "I was in the homecoming court that year, and I remember just how heartbroken we all were and what an impact it made to see the empty senior class float, when the others were so full."[98] A member of the senior class was standing with a friend in front of Brookside dorm during the parade: "I remember the floats coming through, and then our float comes through, empty with just that little church on it, and we just stood there and sobbed."[99]

The original plan was for the senior homecoming queen candidates and their escorts to ride in their horse-drawn carriages to the quad immediately following the parade, where one of them would have been crowned homecoming queen.[100] In the only substantial change to the schedule for homecoming weekend, the ceremony that would crown the queen was cancelled. The men's soccer team took the field against Niagara University at 2:00 p.m. on Saturday, without their co-captain Al. Co-captain Brian Davidson was described as "distraught," trying to play the game without his best friend.[101] Head coach Doug Burke commented: "Each of us carried our own memories into the game."[102] The game ended in a scoreless tie.

Saturday came to a close in Wesley Chapel with the traditional talent and variety show known as "Senate Spot." In the same auditorium where the community had gathered three days earlier to grieve, the campus now gathered to laugh and be entertained by the musical and comedic talents of fellow community members. Even President and Mrs. Chamberlain contributed to the whimsy, as they dressed up again in their Western gear and sang the light-hearted duet, "Anything You Can Do (I Can Do Better)."[103]

The Senate Spot ended on a poignant note with a slide show featuring pictures of Mark, Beth, Alan, Joy, Bert, and Cindy. As the crowd viewed a series of candid photographs of The Six on the huge screen at the front of the auditorium, sophomore student Arlene Francis read a poem called "Homecoming Canceled?" that she had written in their honor:

> Homecoming canceled? Not for you. It came a week early, but still on time. With Father waiting at the gate, the mansion was a pleasant site. So tell me—what was the welcoming parade like? Did the angels wear their finest apparel with beams of the Son reflecting off them? It was probably a sight that 3-D glasses couldn't capture. Oh, and how was the Spot? I imagine the talent was excellent, with uplifting acts of praise in between. I wonder who the host and hostess were. Of course, we all know who the main attraction was—The One and Only Master of our lives. Now, I'm not quite sure if I should ask—but, did you have a soccer game? And did your favorite player make the

> winning goal? I bet you were on the sidelines, cheering him on like you always did before. I guess all this doesn't matter compared to the choosing of the queen. How did it feel to be one of the chosen few, and to be taken for His bride? Homecoming canceled? No, definitely not for you.[104]

Some remember with fondness and appreciation the Spot's closing tribute to the six students; others saw it as premature. "We weren't ready for that yet," one senior recalled.[105]

As the unimaginable and unforgettable week concluded, the college and its students were attempting to come to terms with the magnitude of the loss. Wounds were deep. Grief was profound. Faith was tested. Questions were real. The sense of shock was persistent. The community was reeling. One friend of The Six recalled: "I went to three funerals in five days. I was feeling shaken, fearful, disoriented. I don't know if I've ever felt that thrown off with reality. I remember my mom telling me that it won't last forever, but it was so unsettling. I needed to go home."[106] Another commented: "I don't remember homecoming that year. I skipped almost everything, not wanting to face that reality over and over again."[107]

And yet even in the midst of crushing grief and disorientation, the community had not given in to despair. In a tender article written about his visit to campus for homecoming, a journalist from Buffalo wrote about the men's soccer game: "The surrounding hills were alive with the colors of autumn, and amid the cheering you could tell that Houghton had come to terms with itself."[108] The same reporter, Ray Hill, commented to President Chamberlain, "I've talked to many reporters covering the story, and every one of them has been overwhelmed by the faith they found on your campus."[109] A statement released by the college provided this self-assessment: "The Houghton community is stricken, but finding fresh unity and strength in trouble, anticipating its Easter in that ultimate homecoming awaiting us all."[110] Pastor Mark Abbott commented: "The faith was tested, but it survived the test. When the students asked 'Why?' we didn't try to give any easy answers. The truth is, we do not know why."[111]

There were no answers, but there was hope. As one alumnus recalled: "The college was trying to pull itself together emotionally and spiritually, and it was kind of a marvel. It seemed that in the face of great tragedy, the community was coherent."[112] It hadn't been perfect. And there was still a long way to go. But with deep belief in God, love for one another, and compassion for the families of the six seniors and the driver of the ill-fated truck, Houghton had persevered through the immediate aftermath of its greatest tragedy. It had been rent in two by sorrow, yet simultaneously held together by faith.

Mark Anderson

Mark Anderson and Beth Andes

Beth Andes (center) and a group of Houghton friends

Alan Bushart singing at a Madrigal Dinner

Alan Bushart (in shorts) and co-captain Brian Davidson
carry Coach Doug Burke off the field after a victory

Joy Ellis

Bert Rapp

Bert Rapp (left) and close friend Ed Taylor

Cindy Rudes

The campus of Houghton College in the early 1980s.

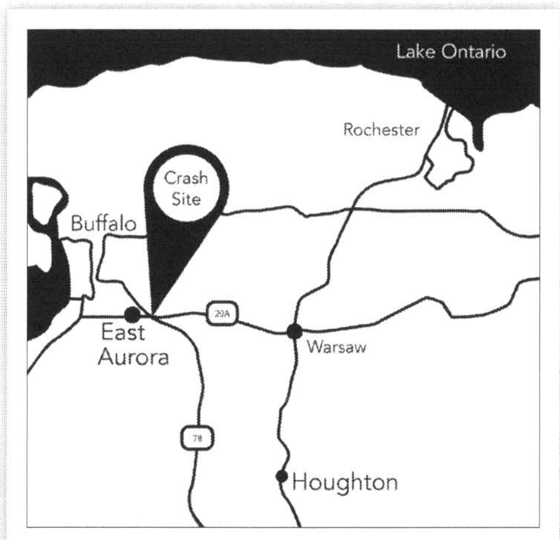

The crash occurred at the intersection of Routes 20A and 78 in the
Town of Wales, approximately 40 miles northwest of Houghton.

Left side of accident site

The photo above, spread across two pages, shows the site of the accident, shortly after the crash, looking east/southeast from Route 20A. The six students approached the intersection from the road on the right, driving northwest on Route 78 (toward the camera). Note the gentle angle at which Route 78 approaches Route 20A. The back of the stop sign on Route 78 is barely visible near the front of the police car

which faces the camera. The tractor trailer was driving eastbound (away from the camera) on Route 20A and is seen on the left at the point at which it came to rest. The students' car (not visible) is in front of the truck under the tree. The photo is taken from the approximate point of impact.

Photo courtesy of Erie County Sheriff's Department.

President Daniel R. Chamberlain being interviewed by Buffalo news media
at the entrance to Wesley Chapel. Students in the background:
Jeff Jordan '83, Tom MacIntyre '83, Mary Beth Fuller Bowling '83, Jack Connell '83.

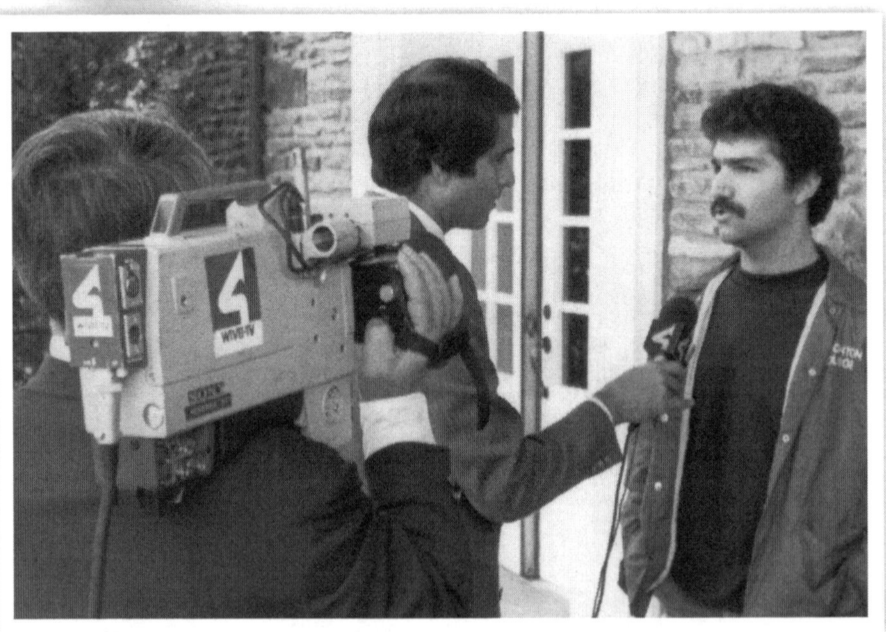

Senior class president Allen Hemayakian being interviewed.

President Chamberlain presides at the campus memorial service.
Seated in the background: Rev. Mark Abbott, pastor of Houghton Wesleyan Church,
and Professor Richard Smiley, senior class advisor.

Campus flag at half mast.

Campus memorial service in Wesley Chapel.

The back of the senior class float in the Homecoming parade.

Dr. and Mrs. Chamberlain sing a duet at the Homecoming Senate Spot.

Robert Danner, dean of student development

Fred Shannon, academic dean

Student Senate cabinet and advisors: Meg Martino, Dr. Katherine Lindley,
Susan Facer (president), Naomi Ruder, Dr. Carl Schultz.

Mercy Zecher Dawson, best friend of Beth Andes,
plays a flute solo at commencement.

Members of the Class of 1982 at graduation.

Installation of the eagles sculpture.

New students gather around the eagles sculpture at the scarf ceremony.

Memorial display in the Kerr-Pegula
Athletic Center that honors the three accident
victims who were student-athletes.

Six eagles soar over the campus today.

EMPTY SEATS
AND FRIDAY FLOWERS

FALL SEMESTER

"I don't think I'll ever stop loving her. I just don't think I ever could. And I'll be honest—a lot of questions are running through my mind. It doesn't make sense."[1] As Joy Ellis' boyfriend struggled to wrap his mind around his loss and imagine the rest of his life without her, so did six bereft families, countless grieving friends, and a campus that tried to move forward with six holes cut into its heart. The first week's tidal wave of grief had been weathered. Now the campus and everyone impacted began to rebuild their lives, their families, and their community.

For the remainder of the semester, reminders of the accident and memories of The Six punctuated each day. As C. S. Lewis said of his beloved wife Joy after her premature death: "Her absence is like the sky, spread over everything."[2] On the Monday or Tuesday after homecoming, a senior student met the local medical doctor while both were walking across campus. The medical doctor was not a young man and was a veteran of many years serving as a medical missionary in Africa; he had seen just about everything life can throw at a person, certainly plenty of death and dying. Yet, as they talked together briefly about the accident, the student noticed the doctor's "grave and saddened demeanor."[3] He was struck by the fact that even someone so much older, who had seen so much suffering, was still rocked by the tragedy.

Students went to classes and other activities and were confronted in many by an empty seat where one of The Six had previously sat. One faculty member suggested to a class that the seats in a particular classroom be rearranged so that the empty spot wouldn't be noticeable and members of the class could "move on." A senior student remembers thinking: "I don't think so! This isn't something you just move on from!"[4] The seat remained empty. In chapel, students sat in assigned seats with faculty members spaced at regular intervals throughout the chapel to check attendance. Seniors were assigned to the front of the chapel that year, and one faculty member had both Cindy Rudes and Joy Ellis in his section. Out of concern that the two empty seats would be a daily reminder of their deaths, the professor kindly gave the other students in the section the freedom to sit elsewhere in chapel for the remainder of the year. The students declined the invitation, and the two seats remained empty.[5] Two seats were also empty at the first Student Senate meeting after the accident—those usually occupied by Mark Anderson and Joy Ellis. A senator for the junior class remembers that during the roll call that opened the meeting "an eerie feeling swept the room as the secretary twice called, 'Proxy for the senior class. Proxy for the senior class.'"[6]

Physical reminders of the departed students confronted the community. Bert Rapp's new car remained parked for a while outside the house near campus where he lived.[7] A faded orange, beat-up backpack that looked like Mark Anderson's lay discarded on the floor in the campus center lounge. A senior student wondered if it could actually be Mark's, opened it up reluctantly, and found pictures of Mark's trip to Alaska inside. It was unmistakably Mark's—presumably left right where he had set it down before getting into the car. The student delivered the backpack to the Dean of Students Office.[8] The Mickey Mouse kite that Joy Ellis flew on the quad remained in a faculty member's home.[9] Spots around campus came to be permanently associated with "where I was when I heard." Soccer games, volleyball matches, orchestra practices, dorm rooms, empty closets—all were tangible reminders of those who were missing. An outing to the Pizza Barn no longer felt like just a carefree evening of pizza and friends and laughter; it was unavoidably also a time of remembering Al and Cindy and all who had been lost.[10]

"The campus felt so heavy, for quite some time."[11] "We were numb, just going through the motions."[12] "To go through something like that at twenty-one was so devastating. We felt this immense sadness and didn't really know what to do with it."[13] "I remember lots of tears—feeling just the utter shock of it all."[14] The four girls who had been housemates with Joy and Cindy largely secluded themselves for the rest of the semester. "We went to class, then went back to the house. And we cried a lot. That's all we could handle."[15]

Yet there was also a tangible sense of mutual support and care; the campus was grieving as a community. Close friends of The Six remember how people they didn't even know came up to them and expressed concern and support. "There was a closeness across the campus. We were all struggling with the same thing."[16] "We grieved and drew closer together."[17] "It brought the campus together in a way that no other event could have, in a way that you don't want to have to happen, but it certainly gelled the campus."[18] A retired faculty member who was particularly close to Mark Anderson reflected: "The response embodied what Houghton was all about. We talk about this being a personal campus, and people were getting together to pray, people were trying to help each other deal with the shock and grief in a very personal way. It was Houghton at its best."[19]

Dr. Chamberlain resumed his more typical presidential duties in the days following homecoming—a fund-raising trip to Pennsylvania, a meeting of Christian college presidents in Washington, DC. In a letter written to his family on October 12, he reflected on the memorial service for the students: "I have never had a more difficult assignment. . . . I knew them all and loved and respected them as did their family and peers. Many had prayed and were praying that I would have special strength for the occasion and I was able to complete the meditation without a major break. The fact that each of these students had a close relationship with Christ, and their faith was vital and well known, made the service triumphant."[20] On October 15, Dr. Chamberlain wrote personal letters of condolence to each of the six sets of parents, in which he included a tape of the memorial service, the addresses and phone numbers of the six families, and the October 9 commemorative issue of the *Houghton Star*. His letter to Mr. and Mrs. Anderson began: "Let me express again in this more formal and official way the deep sense of loss we share with you in Mark's sudden homegoing. He was loved by us all and we will miss the ready smile, the radiant faith, and the many contributions to campus life." Chamberlain continued: "While we sorrow at Mark's passing, we rejoice with complete assurance that he is with the Lord he loved and served. Heaven has been enriched and our resolve has been strengthened to run faithfully the race before us until we are again united where sorrow and separation are forever past."[21]

Dr. Chamberlain's letters arrived at the homes of moms and dads and siblings who were each trying in their own ways to cope with the suffocating intensity of their grief. At first, Mr. and Mrs. Rudes did not intend to return to their missionary work in Indonesia. They did not want to leave their remaining daughter, Debbie, alone in the United States to deal with the loss of her only sister. Later in October, Debbie's boyfriend asked Mr. Rudes for Debbie's hand in marriage. Now knowing that Debbie would have the companionship of a spouse, Mr. and Mrs. Rudes felt free to return to Indonesia and did so on October 31. Debbie struggled with survivor's guilt. She said: "Cindy was headed to the mission field. Her faith was always stronger than mine, she was less emotionally needy than I was. She was going to be a missionary, and I was just going to be me, a school teacher. So I had a lot of guilt about that." Speaking of her parents' grief, Debbie said: "People tend to either run to God or run away from God. My parents definitely ran to God, although I know my mom in particular struggled so much."[22] Her parents' faith is evident in the Scripture verse with which they closed their November 1981 letter to prayer partners and financial supporters: "We are not our own bosses to live or die as we ourselves might choose. Living or dying we follow the Lord. Either way we are his. Christ died and rose again for this very purpose, so that he can be our Lord while we live and when we die" (Rom. 14:7–9 TLB).[23] Since Cindy died on a Friday, Mr. Rudes attempted to console his wife by bringing her flowers every Friday in the years that followed.[24]

Mark Anderson's brother Terry remembers that Mark's death was "devastating for my parents. They placed so much love and hope in their kids." Shortly after Mark's funeral, Mr. and Mrs. Anderson left their home in Connecticut and drove across the country for three months—thousands of miles of talking, getting space, visiting friends, and grieving. Terry said: "That extended time away gave them a certain amount of coming to terms with the loss—but thirty years later, they would still weep. Their lives were changed forever." Terry compared their loss to a dog that loses a leg: "In time they can learn to get along fairly well, but they're really hobbling and missing that leg. My parents always had that space in their lives." Of his own grief, Terry said: "Maybe because of my New England roots, it took me a long time to process it all—the sadness of missing him, the sadness of what might have been."[25] Mark's brother Keith returned to work at the hospital about a week after Mark's death "because there was nothing else I could do; I was just a zombie at that point." "For a long time," he commented, "I missed him every day. He was my closest friend."[26]

In the days leading up to Beth's funeral, the Andes family was inundated with people eager to offer support and comfort—people from the Pottstown community, from Beth's high school, from their church, and from Houghton. In the days after the funeral, like the Andersons, they found themselves needing solitude. Consequently, Mr. and Mrs. Andes took their two remaining daughters and son-in-law into the Pennsylvania mountains for some extended time together as family. Beth's sister Mindy recalls: "We got away from all the people and all the voices and we just pressed into each other and into God. It was wisdom on the part of my parents that we did this, because more than anything, that time away provided a foundation for us as a family to be able to move forward. It was a time that allowed God to minister to us on a very deep level." Permeating their time together was the deep trust in God that Mr. and Mrs. Andes displayed: "They showed us that we can trust God despite the trauma we are experiencing. That God is here, that he never leaves us or forsakes us, and that there will be good that comes out of this because that's who God is. I saw their quiet strength, despite the grieving." Mindy went on to say, though, that Mr. Andes was never quite the same man after he lost his youngest daughter. "He experienced profound, deep grief, and it changed him. It took some of the vitality out of his life, and it never really came back."[27]

For months after Alan's funeral, Mr. Bushart would sit quietly and listen over and over to the audio recording of the service. He was in agony over the loss of his son and was questioning God: "I'm old and I'm not well. How could God allow this to happen?" He didn't reject God, and in time his questions eased, but in the early days, his faith was severely tested. Mr. and Mrs. Bushart tried, as much as possible, to continue with activities that would keep Alan's memory alive—attending Houghton soccer games and keeping in close contact with his friends. They retired shortly thereafter, having been reminded that life is very short. Warren and Barb Bushart came back to Houghton and reopened the Pizza Barn, but it was awkward and difficult. "People stayed away because they were unsure of what to say to us," Barb said. "It definitely affected our business. And everyone who did come in would begin to cry." They closed the Pizza Barn about a year later. Barb, an ordained minister, later preached a sermon on how people tend to respond with harshness to the fear and dejection the disciples felt after Jesus' death. "But that's how I felt after Al died," she said. "I was just undone."[28]

Nearly 5000 miles away in Hawaii, Rob Jacobsen, a recent Houghton graduate and friend of all six, was sitting in the stairwell of the YMCA in which he lived about two weeks after the accident. As was his custom, Rob was using the stairwell as a quiet place to reflect on Scripture and work on songwriting. With the deaths of his friends much on his mind, Rob opened his Bible to Isaiah 40:27–31, a passage that acknowledges the human propensity to ask questions of God in the face of suffering, transitions to trust in the transcendent wisdom of God, and then concludes with buoyant confidence that those whose hope is in the Lord "will soar on wings like eagles." A progression of chords came to Rob quickly and easily: "It felt more like I heard it than wrote it." And in one session in the echoey stairwell, Rob wrote most of the song called, "Do You Not Know?" that would in coming months become an anthem of hope for the grieving Houghton community. What Rob did not know at the time is that Isaiah 40:31 was the verse selected by the class of 1982 as their class verse.[29]

Isaiah 40:31 reads as follows: "Those who hope in the LORD will renew their strength. They will soar on wings like eagles; they will run and not grow weary, they will walk and not be faint." Back on campus as the fall semester continued, the thought of soaring on wings like eagles probably seemed too aspirational. Even running and not growing weary was optimistic. The more reasonable goal for the final weeks of the semester was Isaiah's more modest one: to walk and not be faint. Students struggled to stay on top of their studies as they grappled with lack of focus, motivation, and purpose. Some remember faculty members pushing them harder than they thought was appropriate; others remember assignments and tests that were graciously postponed or cancelled. A senior music major who needed to postpone her senior recital to the spring semester commented, "I honestly don't know how I got through the rest of the semester."[30] Another member of the senior class remembered: "I think the deaths did contribute on some level to a lack of motivation my senior year and to wondering what was the point of ANY human effort in light of our mortality. . . . Academically, I found myself caring less."[31] One said candidly: "My classes suffered terribly."[32]

Students understandably grappled in late-night discussions and in their own quiet moments with innumerable questions about what had happened. Countless contingencies had aligned so tragically at the intersection of Routes 20A and 78. What if the students had chosen a different route? Or stopped for coffee? Or taken a different car? What if the truck driver had lingered for thirty more seconds as he said good-bye to his wife? Some of the contingencies were more personal. The vote for the homecoming queen nominees was very close, with only one vote separating the third-place finisher (who was selected) from the fourth-place finisher (who was not). At least one member of the senior class pondered at length how a change in his vote could have potentially saved one girl her life and cost another hers.[33] Other seniors likely had similar musings.

A friend of Joy's remembers a conversation the week before the accident in which Joy named the friends she was considering as her escort; Bert was one of a handful of possibilities at that point. In the days and weeks after the accident, the friend remembers seeing the men who Joy did not choose and thinking to herself, *You could be dead right now and you don't even know it.*[34] The senior class president, Allen Hemayakian, who backed out of the Buffalo trip due to an afternoon exam, struggled with nagging guilt. "Had I gone, the whole thing could have changed completely. We would have traveled in a different manner, and the accident may not have happened. Or we would have been in two cars and some would have been spared. I was in a daze for a long time about all of this."[35] Hemayakian's best friend, Tim Nichols, had been on the senior homecoming court the previous year. The memories of his own participation on the homecoming court combined with his best friend's near miss created a confluence of questions and contingencies that was "this crushing thing I had to wrestle with."[36] Many were engaged in the same wrestling match. Was it God's will that it all happened this way? Was this part of some grand design? If so, why? Or was it all just a series of random coincidences? Or some of both? And how will we ever know?

Student Senate president Sue Facer commented at the time: "I don't want to say we don't ask 'why?', because we do. Houghton is distinctive for being a

Christian college, but it's also stressed the liberal arts education. We are taught not to dismiss questions but to think them through."[37] In addition to all the "why" questions, some students wondered about the nature of the hope that was talked about so frequently on campus: Is this hope the same thing as certainty? What exactly is it that we are hoping for? "And how did any one person's spiritual state enter into the equation of our hope?"[38] Others wondered about the nature of the afterlife: "Is there really a heaven, and how do we know if they are there?"[39] And of course, there were all the questions about what might have been for The Six, who were so filled with promise—what kind of people would they have become? What kind of difference would they have made in the world? As Glenn Burlingame, a close friend of Mark Anderson, commented, "That is the hardest thing about looking at lives cut short—the whole future is gone."[40]

The Student Life staff, led by dean of students Robert Danner, worked tirelessly to serve and support students through their questions, doubts, and struggles. But the staff was small. And in the early 1980s, there was less awareness of the need for grief counselors and support structures and small groups and seminars and other types of programming that would have provided students with more coping tools. In the absence of those resources, Danner's staff did the very best they could. Dr. Chamberlain commented, "Bob Danner was a tower of strength and wisdom. I have thanked the Lord at least a thousand times that Bob was here during that time."[41]

The campus organizations to which The Six belonged attempted to move forward without their senior leaders. The men's soccer team admirably played out its season without its co-captain, but could understandably manage only an 8–7–3 record, subpar for Houghton's distinguished soccer program. The yearbook's description of their season included an allusion to the song that provided the title for the senior class float: "Through it all, the guys bonded together to lend hugs, tears, words of comfort, and encouragement to one another. They united with determination to complete the season, giving it their all."[42] The women's volleyball team had a similarly challenging season without Cindy (and without Joy, who had previously decided not to play her senior season), but the young team finished with a respectable record of 14–16. The yearbook noted: "Throughout the season and especially because of the tragic loss of their captain, Cindy Rudes, the girls grew closer together and learned to support one another. As a result, they matured as players."[43] As the vice president of the Young Administrators Organization, I (Jack) was daunted and overwhelmed by the expectation that I would step into Bert's role as president. I did the best I could.

The November issue of the college alumni magazine featured an article about the accident called "Tragedy, Triumph and the Ultimate Homecoming." Accompanying the article were photos of the intersection, the memorial service, Dr. Chamberlain being interviewed by a journalist, and the senior class float. In his editorial byline, Dean Liddick provided his perspective about the campus: "Repeatedly, reporters expressed surprise, puzzlement, and a kind of admiration over the way the campus drew together, managed crushing sorrow, tasteful commemoration, and resolute continuity of program, all in a week. Such a profound witness didn't just happen, nor was it the result of a 'let's pull up our socks and get on with it' stoicism. Rather it was the considered result of a permeating Christian faith."[44] Next to a stark photo of the campus flag at half-staff was a poem that Professor Jack Leax had read in chapel days after the accident. Called "Canticles Autumn" by Arnold Kenseth, the poem begins with these words: "Lord, all is ready. Our hearts wait. Earth brims to its dying."[45] Words of tribute and photos of the six students concluded the prominent section of the magazine devoted to the accident.

As the fall semester came to a close, the campus received another shock. On December 9, Mark Schiefer, a student at the Buffalo Suburban Campus who had previously been a student on the main campus, was killed in a wintry car accident less than ten miles from the site of the October 2 accident.[46] Like Cindy Rudes, his parents were missionaries in the Far East. Perhaps never before in Houghton's history had a Christmas break been more needed, yet so fraught with tangled questions and frazzled emotions. Students and their families surely cherished some extended time together to rest and remember and ponder the coming of the Christ child; it was an Advent season of reflecting on the mysteries of faith and being grateful for the fragile gift of life. The six (now seven) bereaved families surely leaned heavily on one another and yearned for the comfort of God as, with heavy hearts, they navigated their first Christmas without their son or daughter, brother or sister.

SPRING SEMESTER

Steve Dunbar, a senior business major and close friend of Bert's, had spent the fall semester at the Buffalo Suburban Campus while he did an internship at a large commercial bank. He was eager to return to the main campus for spring semester so that he could "be surrounded by the Houghton community." His original plan was to room with Bert for their final semester before graduation, in the off-campus home of Bert's sister and brother-in-law. He accepted their kind invitation to stay there in spite of Bert's death and remembers, "It was good for all of us as we drew strength from one another."[47] Drawing strength from one another was a project for the entire campus that spring, as students, faculty, and staff came to terms with what had happened and regained a greater degree of equilibrium. President Chamberlain recalled that the healing on campus "was not at all instantaneous, but was a long process"—and that process of grieving and healing continued throughout the spring.[48]

As part of that healing process, some students made the pilgrimage to the intersection where the accident had occurred. They wanted to drive the last few miles their friends had driven, see what they had seen, and imagine their final moments together. They wanted to stand silently at the strange, oblique intersection, look at the awkward lines of sight and grieve what had happened there. One friend of The Six remembers feeling deeply ministered to by God while there.[49] Others wanted to avoid the intersection at all costs and always made sure that any trip to Buffalo took a route that missed the Town of Wales.

The house in which Joy, Cindy, and four other seniors lived was owned by Tom Kettlekamp—a faculty member who was away with his wife on sabbatical for the entire year. Consequently, Professor Kettlekamp did not know the senior girls particularly well; they were simply the students who were renting his house while he was away. At some point before the end of the spring semester, both Cindy's parents and Joy's parents mailed to the Kettlekamps the rent that they would have paid for the remainder of the academic year. Apparently, both families were concerned that the Kettlekamps not incur any financial hardship as a result of their daughters' deaths. Joy was a pastor's kid. Cindy was a missionary's kid. Neither family had significant financial resources, and when the Kettlekamps received these checks, Tom recalled, "We just sat down and wept." As he told me the story, more than forty years later, he began to weep again: "What a kind, generous gesture that was. We couldn't believe it." Gathering himself, he added: "Of course, we didn't keep the money; there's no way we could have done that."[50]

In another expression of the parents' generosity with the Houghton community, the Rapps gave Bert's college ring to his girlfriend, Karyn Hecht. They would return to campus a year later and give her a flowered china bowl as a graduation present.[51]

Spring came to upstate New York toward the end of the semester, and the quad began to fill again with ultimate frisbee games and study groups. The baseball, softball, and track teams completed their seasons. Students hustled to finish term papers and study for final exams. The campus gathered for the typical array of year-end banquets and concerts. And the senior class, now smaller by six, made sure their graduation requirements were fulfilled and finalized their post-graduation plans; some seniors whose grief was especially intense struggled to complete their coursework and were dependent upon concessions made by empathetic faculty members. As was tradition, the senior class was placed in charge of the final chapel of the year. A popular song at the time called "Arthur's Theme" contained this line: "When you get caught between the moon and New York City, the best that you can do is fall in love." The class of 1982 smiled and laughed as they sang the song with that line revised for Houghton's unique location: "When you get caught between Hume and Caneadea, the best that you can do is get a job."[52] Although The Six remained much on their minds, joy was beginning to return.

On Monday, May 10, Houghton College held its 82nd annual commencement for the class of 1982. Seven months after the community packed into Wesley Chapel for a memorial service in honor of the six seniors who were lost, the chapel was filled again to celebrate the achievements of the 228 who remained. Before the presentation of degrees, senior class president Allen Hemayakian was invited to the podium, where he announced a gift that the senior class had voted to give to the college: "As most of you know, we lost six of our classmates earlier this year in a tragic car accident. Instead of being with us at this time, these friends are with our heavenly Father. Surely in a sense they are rejoicing with us right now, and perhaps even more important, we are looking forward to the day when we will join them in that more complete rejoicing around God's throne. But until that day comes, we want to honor our six friends with a permanent memorial here on our campus. The class of 1982 is purchasing for the college six outdoor benches to be located around the campus. Each bench will carry a plaque with the name of one our friends."[53]

On behalf of the college, President Chamberlain gratefully received the gift. "Thank you, Allen, and thank you members of the senior class. Words and gifts can never express how much we loved and respected these six young people, and how much we have missed them. They challenged us by their vibrant Christian lives, and they brought us closer to God and to each other by their sudden passing. They live on in our hearts as surely as they do in God's nearer presence. This gift is a permanent and appropriate way to perpetuate their individual memories and witness to the fact that they are a permanent part of the Houghton College community. Thank you again, Allen and seniors."

Dr. Chamberlain then made this announcement: "You will notice in your program that we have by action of the faculty and the Board of Trustees conferred posthumous degrees on these six young people. So Mark Anderson, Beth Andes, Alan Bushart, Joy Ellis, Bert Rapp and Cindy Rudes are all graduates of Houghton College as of today." About ten members of the six families were in attendance, and Dr. Chamberlain invited them to stand so that the graduates and the entire congregation could express to them their welcome and love.[54] As they stood, Wesley Chapel reverberated with a loud and extended round of applause for them.

After receiving their degrees, the members of the class of 1982 spilled out onto the portico and into the quad to say farewell to faculty members and one another. Yearbook photos capture some smiling, some in conversation, and some in pensive reflection as they stand in the sunshine together. In the days immediately after the accident, a journalist who visited Houghton had written: "College prepares students for life, not death."[55] The members of Houghton College's class of 1982 must have believed they had been prepared for both.

The yearbook for the 1981–82 academic year was released a few weeks after graduation. The 1982 *Boulder* (its name an echo of the college's motto "Founded on the Rock") opens with several pages of campus photos from the year: athletic contests, smiling students with big '80s hair, the quad blanketed by snow, a faculty member proudly holding his new baby, the mascot highlander playing the bagpipes. The next page contains only these words: "To the Glory of God and in Memory of Mark Bertram Anderson, Beth Renee Andes, Alan Robert Bushart, Joy Suzanne Ellis, Albert Lester Rapp, Cynthia Rae Rudes." A full-page photo of the campus flag at half-staff comes next, with the title "The Final Homecoming" and a brief synopsis of the accident and the community's love for The Six. Three pages of joy-filled photos of The Six follow: Mark sitting in the driver's seat of his yellow taxi in Alaska; Beth intently playing her flute; Alan smiling as he sings at a Madrigal dinner; Cindy and Joy laughing together at the beach on a spring break trip to Florida; Bert looking like a happy young executive in his three-piece suit and dark tie. The photos speak of their life, their joy, their vitality, their promise. Interspersed among the many photos are excerpts from the words of tribute that Dr. Chamberlain offered at the memorial service: "his warmth and honesty," "she was always ready to pray with others," "he lived his life as an open book," "the lovely, ladylike attitude of a young woman whose heart belonged to Jesus Christ," "a leader of others," "the Christ-centered joy that enabled her to take difficulties in stride."

The memorial section of the 1982 yearbook concludes with a photo of an empty bench on an empty quad: an image of loneliness and loss. Superimposed on the photo are the words of a prayer written by Pastor Abbott:

> *Thank You, Father of Life, for the memories of*
> *their beauty and strength,*
> *their smiles and good humor,*
> *their scholarship and spirituality,*
> *their talents and skills.*
> *Thank You, Heavenly Father, for their witness by life and through death.*
> *Thank You, God of Truth, for questions about their death;*
> *Questions which cause us to reexamine*
> *and review*
> *and reaffirm*
> *our commitment to You and our understanding of life and death.*
> *Thank You, God of all comfort,*

for grief that is shared,
for comfort experienced together,
for hope which we share as a community.
Thank You, God of strength, for courage not to be overwhelmed by sadness;
But rather, for courage to live life to its fullest as they did,
true to their memory,
true to our covenant with You,
true to our sure hope of joining them in Your nearer presence.
Amen.[56]

It had been a year like no other.

MAKING SENSE OF SUFFERING

How does one find peace in the face of a thousand empty tomorrows? How does one find meaning amid soul-crushing loss? How does one make sense of the senseless? Upon hearing the news of his wife's tragic and untimely death, Shakespeare's MacBeth offered his thoughts on the matter: "Life's but a walking shadow, a poor player that struts and frets his hour upon the stage, and then is heard no more. It is a tale told by an idiot, full of sound and fury, signifying nothing."[1] Philosophers, poets, and ordinary people have arrived at a similar conclusion: that the seemingly random and chaotic way in which suffering ricochets around our world, striking some people and sparing others, renders life essentially meaningless. Others take a different view and see a perfectly ordered world in which everything that happens is prescribed by God and is in accordance with his wisdom and plan. One finds hints of this worldview in the majestic hymn I first learned at Houghton, "Like a River Glorious": "Every joy or trial falleth from above, / Traced upon our dial by the Sun of Love. / We may trust Him fully, all for us to do; / They who trust Him wholly find Him wholly true."[2] Many land somewhere between MacBeth and the hymnwriter, trying to find a worldview that accounts for both a sovereign God and the messiness of life in a fallen world.

The scope and complexity of these questions extends far beyond the boundaries of this small book and the modest capabilities of its author. All I intend to do in this final chapter is provide snapshots of how the college itself and some of the individuals most deeply impacted by the events of October 2, 1981, wrestled with these questions and tried to find meaning in what happened that day. I am not attempting to develop a conceptual framework for dealing with grief. Or find a solution to the problem of evil. Or adjudicate the disagreements between Christians who emphasize divine determinism and those who focus on human free will. Or answer the many questions about God and faith and life and death that still reverberate from the accident. I simply intend to share the voices of a variety of people of faith connected to one Christian college as they have lived with and tried to come to terms with what happened. My purpose is not to analyze or critique their thoughts and experiences; it is not my place or intention to make value judgments about how people grieve or think about suffering. I simply offer their perspectives and stories, with the hope that by the grace of God you might find something that will be helpful as you reflect on suffering and loss in your own life. "In this world you will have trouble," Jesus said (John 16:33). Yet Christ invites us to "take heart" in the face of that trouble. Can people actually do that? How?

COLLEGE COMMEMORATIONS

The accident was so searingly consequential in the life of the college that it became evident almost immediately that it needed to be permanently commemorated on campus. The idea of a campus sculpture emerged during the 1981–82 academic year and was endorsed by the Student Senate that same year.[3] A variety of proposals were considered formally and informally over the next couple of years, but none received strong support from the college administration and students. One proposal called for six tombstones, each inscribed with the name and dates of birth and death of one of the students. "It was horrible," Dr. Chamberlain recalled of the proposal. "We needed something that would be honoring to God and recognize our eternal life with him."[4]

In 1984, Chamberlain learned that the father of a new Houghton student was a sculptor whose work was displayed in a number of prominent places throughout the eastern United States—from Callaway Gardens in Georgia to

Harvard University.[5] The sculptor, David Caccia of Sewell, New Jersey, met with Dr. Chamberlain and the idea of a sculpture based on the soaring eagles of the senior class verse arose out of their conversations. Mr. Caccia had sculpted birds most of his life, and for this project, watched videos of eagles in flight and studied the golden eagles at the Philadelphia Zoo. "I knew it had to be a large piece," he said. "The nature of the accident dictated that." He ultimately proposed a twenty-foot-high sculpture that would feature life-sized eagles with wingspans that are six feet across. The concept was approved by the college and took sixteen months to complete. Mr. Caccia said he would consider the sculpture his greatest work "if the parents of the victims find comfort in the statue when they see it."[6]

The bronze sculpture was erected on campus in the summer of 1986. Located in front of the Reinhold Campus Center (where The Six had gathered for their trip), adjacent to the quad, and surrounded by the six benches that were the graduation gifts of the class of 1982, its prominent place on campus reflects the significance of the event in the life of the college, as well as the central place of the lost students in the heart of the community. The sculpture was dedicated during homecoming weekend on October 11, 1986, the five-year anniversary of the homecoming of tears.

Family members of The Six and the campus community gathered around the sculpture as Dr. Chamberlain made the dedicatory remarks. Reflecting on the six who were lost, he said, "They were precious to us in their lives and leadership." Chamberlain then spoke about the Christian convictions about eternity that inspired the concept of the sculpture: "Our secular society has attempted to make death individual, private, and utterly final. Secularists have tried to hide death and thus deny it—or to regard death as the ultimate proof of futility. But as Christians we know better; we know that earthly life is the prelude to eternal life. And so I asked the artist to prepare a model that expressed life; a work that would lift our eyes in faith and hope to heaven. This sculpture symbolizes not only these six students, but also the fundamental and enduring purposes of life. We are firmly planted on earth, but we are meant to fly—to soar as eagles in spirit and to spend an eternity with our Creator." Then, reprising the closing words of his message at the campus memorial service five years earlier, Chamberlain said: "I pray this sculpture will be for all of us a constant reminder that our lives are valued for the relationships we established with God and others, and that the impact of our lives is the result of the quality of those relationships, not the number of our days. May we remember that for Christians it is never 'farewell'; it is always 'till we meet again.'"[7]

Dr. Chamberlain unveiled the bronze plaque that was installed next to the sculpture: "'They shall mount up with wings as eagles . . .' Dedicated to the six students killed in a car accident. October 2, 1981. Mark Anderson, Beth Andes, Alan Bushart, Joy Ellis, Albert Rapp, Cynthia Rudes. David A. Caccia, Sculptor." Concluding his comments, Dr. Chamberlain said, "Even as we dedicate this sculpture, let us rededicate ourselves to the qualities and commitments exhibited by Mark, Beth, Alan, Joy, Bert, and Cindy, so that every earthly homecoming will renew our longing and readiness for the ultimate homecoming."

The eagles sculpture and six surrounding benches have become for many a sacred and deeply emotional place of remembrance on campus. A classmate of The Six commented, "I can't look up at the eagles memorial and read the names on the benches without some sort of tears."[8] Her voice cracking with emotion, an alumna who was a junior in 1981 said, "Whenever I go back to Houghton, it still breaks my heart to see the eagles and the benches."[9] Another classmate describes the difficulty of returning to campus: "Forty years later it still chokes me up. It's just too hard—the benches, the sculpture, it brings it all back."[10] A retired administrator describes the sculpture as "a holy place on campus."[11]

Dr. Robert Danner, the dean of students at the time of the tragedy, worked at the college until his retirement many years later, and walked by the soaring eagles innumerable times over the course of his career. Sometimes he would walk past the sculpture and hardly notice it, preoccupied with the responsibilities and challenges of the day. "But then I would walk by it on another day and," Danner said, pausing to collect himself, "and I couldn't even walk by. I'd have to stand there and get myself together, because there were these six wonderful kids that are gone; their lives cut short. Maybe not in God's sense, but in a human sense. They had their whole lives ahead of them, and they're gone now. And I'd be standing on the sidewalk looking at the eagles and someone would say to me, 'Are you OK?' because tears would be streaming down my face."[12]

Almost ten years to the day after the accident, the Houghton community was rocked by another tragedy when two students were killed in a car accident.

Dr. Bud Bence, a Houghton alumnus and academic dean at the time, spoke at the campus memorial service for Jim Francis Jr. and Paul Maxwell. "After the service, I recall walking to the eagles and the six benches in front of the campus center. My immediate grief expanded to enclose all those individuals whose lives were cut too short by their passing while students at Houghton. Those who left the classroom to die on battlefields in defense of our country. Others succumbed to illness and disease long before they approached their prime. And yes, there were a few who found the stresses of life so unbearable that they took matters into their own hands. But then a moment of stillness, under the wings of the eagles, in the shadow of the Almighty, I found what Irish monks ages ago described as a 'thin place'—a spot where the realities of a kingdom to come seem somehow closer and arrive almost to the touching point with the harsh realities of this fallen world. There, in quiet reflection, I reached out to the six students whose names adorned the benches and to scores of others whose brief sojourn on Houghton's campus impacted their lives, and ours, for good."[13]

The eagles sculpture ensured that the six lost in 1981 would never be far from the college's consciousness, but on the twenty-fifth anniversary of the accident, Houghton brought the accident into the foreground and reflected on its meaning for a new generation of community members. On October 2, 2006, Houghton invited family members of The Six back to campus for a commemorative chapel service and luncheon. Three of the mothers attended—Jane Andes, Isabel Bushart, and Carol Ellis—along with several siblings and family members. They were joined in worship by several hundred members of the Houghton community, the vast majority of whom did not know The Six—students who were not even born in 1981—and faculty and staff who had mostly come to Houghton in the years since 1981.[14]

In her words of welcome, associate professor of religion Kristina LaCelle-Peterson, a classmate of The Six, said:

"We celebrate their lives today because we're part of something much bigger than your four years here. We are part of an eternal community. We are part of a church. We're part of a community that's founded by a God who never forgets, by a God whose love never ends. Even if you didn't know these

> people, they're a part of us." Her opening prayer included these words: "We thank you for the way you've created our hearts, which is for love. Thank you that you created us capable of deep joy, deep love, even if it means deep sorrow. . . . Help us to know that you are not surprised or scared by our grief. Or irritated by the length of it. . . . Give us a glimpse of a life where there is no loss, where there are no tears, where we sit down in joy with those who have gone before us."

Other features of the service included slides of campus life in the early 1980s and photos of The Six, a musical duet by Scott and Mercy Zecher Dawson from the class of 1982, and a performance by the chamber singers of "Brother James' Air," which was sung by the college choir at the memorial service in 1981.

The sermon was delivered by Rev. Dr. J. Michael Walters, who had followed Mark Abbott as pastor of the Houghton Wesleyan Church and later joined the Houghton faculty as professor of religion. Walters related to the congregation that he had prepared his sermon while looking at the eagles sculpture from the vantage points provided by the six benches, and that his thoughts had coalesced around ideas from two Scripture passages. First, as Pastor Abbott had done the Sunday after the accident, Walters spoke about the brevity and uncertainty of life from James 4: "James' words confront our death-denying culture with the cold hard truth that life comes with no guarantees, that even the youngest, strongest and most vital among us are mist-like and temporal." In response to the "why" question which "has hung over this campus for twenty-five years," Walters acknowledged the lack of a definitive answer. "There are times when the words 'I don't know' are more than an admission of ignorance; there are times when such words are a submission to our creatureliness and a confession that in the end we are dependent upon something beyond ourselves. To those six eagles forever suspended in flight over this campus, I ultimately repeat six times: I don't know."

Walters then turned the congregation's attention to Romans 8:39: Nothing "will be able to separate us from the love of God that is in Christ Jesus our Lord." He commented, "October 2, 1981, was perhaps Houghton's worst day ever. But the pain of that terrible day is made bearable by the promise of the gospel; the horror of the past is overcome by the hope of the future. The pain is real, the scars are deep, but in the end, love wins. Our lives are vaporous and fleeting, but they are held precious in some deeper eternal sense by the God of the universe. . . . The last word belongs to God." Walters concluded his message with these direct words to the students in the audience: "Hear me well, my seemingly indestructible twenty-something brothers and sisters. Life comes with no guarantees. No guarantees except this huge asterisk that is ours by faith. We stand here today like candles in the wind—vulnerable, subject to the sudden swirls of the human condition. But we also stand here by faith as children of the heavenly Father."

The service concluded with Rob and Wendy Jacobsen, schoolmates and friends of The Six, leading the congregation in the song that Rob had written in the stairwell of a YMCA building in Hawaii two weeks after the accident. As it had many times in the twenty-five years since the accident, Wesley Chapel was filled with the sound of voices singing: "Do you not know? Have you not heard? The Lord is the everlasting God. . . . Those who hope in the Lord will renew their strength. They will soar on wings like eagles, they will run and not grow weary, they will walk and not be faint." At the conclusion of the service, family members attended a luncheon in the Reinhold Campus Center. Afterward, many of them lingered around the eagles sculpture for a time of reflection and remembering.[15]

In an essay for Houghton's alumni magazine commemorating the twenty-fifth anniversary, Tim Nichols wrote of the day of the accident: "We discovered that day that the world was a dark and dangerous place and that God didn't seem to be watching out for us in quite the way we'd always imagined. That day, we felt the way Senator Daniel Moynihan did after the assassination of President Kennedy: 'Yes, we'll laugh again, but we'll never be young again.' . . . We have few answers, but of this we are certain: the same loving arms that received our friends will one day embrace us as well. Their deaths remind us that it could be a generation from now, or it could be tomorrow. We are also certain of this: we are not made for this earth, but for eternity. And we have this final hope, made certain by our Lord Jesus Christ: the sadness that we have over the loss of our friends will fall away, replaced with joy, at our homecoming reunion in the glorious world that is to come."[16]

Three years later, in the fall of 2009, the Houghton administration began a new tradition intended to connect current students to the history of the eagles sculpture and the significance of the accident. On November 11, the members of the freshman class gathered around the eagles sculpture for a candlelight service. They were told the story of the six students who were killed and of the ways in which the Houghton community came together in the wake of the tragedy to support and comfort the stricken families and one another. Each new student was then presented with a Houghton scarf and assured that their own journey through Houghton—the joys and difficulties—would not be undertaken alone but would instead be surrounded by the embrace of that loving, supportive community. As an expression of their appreciation for that community, the students were encouraged to give their scarf away at some point before they graduated to a member of the community who had supported them in an especially meaningful way. The scarf ceremony has been held for new students each year since its inception, and although minor modifications have been made, it continues to reflect the purposes for which it was started: "It is our hope that this tradition will help the memories of the six Houghton students and the message of the eagles sculpture to endure, and for us to continue to foster the type of community described following the tragedy of 1981."[17]

I had the privilege of speaking at the scarf ceremony when I served as Houghton's provost from 2016–2019. I struggled for days to find words that would communicate to these young men and women the sacredness of each person and the eternal value of their relationships with one another. Again, I did the best I could, and said in part:

> You know, students, we live in a funny world. We're always so busy doing our usual things, but then every once in a while, something happens—a hurricane devastates a community, or a child goes missing, or a soccer team in Thailand gets trapped in a flooded cave. Or a car accident takes the lives of six of our friends. And suddenly, we're stopped in our tracks and we remember what really matters. It's like the scales fall from our eyes, and we see in those moments what God sees with perfect clarity all the time: the immeasurable value of each

person on the planet. Each one loved by God and made in his image and died for by his Son; each one a sacred gift.[18] You are surrounded by your fellow students tonight—many of them already friends, many more who will become your friends—and you get to do life with them for these four brief years. We'd rather it didn't take a tragedy like October 2, 1981, to remind you what a gift they are and what a gift this community is. So, when you sit on these benches and walk by these eagles and wear these scarves, we hope you will do so not with despair or sadness, but with wonder and reverence for the gift God has given you in one another.

Shirley A. Mullen served as Houghton's president from 2006 to 2021, and recently reflected on the significance of the accident and the eagles statue in Houghton's history:

I was in graduate school in Minnesota when I first heard about the tragic accident that resulted in the death of six members of Houghton's class of 1982. My brother was in the class of 1982, and my father was on the faculty at the time. Even hearing the news from a distance, I understood how devastating this would be for the families involved and for the entire Houghton community.

Whenever I returned to Houghton between 1981 and 2006 to visit family, I would hear bits and pieces of the story and ongoing implications of the tragedy. I was pleased when Houghton chose to create a monument to the event—thus making it forever part of our institutional memory. The monument was placed intentionally in a place that was highly visible and directly in the line of heavy student traffic. Anyone passing the eagles would be compelled to ask, in the tradition of Joshua 4, "What does this statue mean?"

So, I understood cognitively the depth of this event long before returning to the campus as Houghton's fifth president in

2006. Furthermore, by that time, I had experienced firsthand the existential impact of a tragedy of similar proportion when I was working at another Christian college. I was beginning to learn that a college community will be forever changed by an event such as had happened in 1981. Everyone who was at Houghton at the time—faculty, staff, student—will carry the scar of that event in their memory. It will be part of their Houghton story. This is especially true for the students—whose entire Houghton story is, at most, four years. For these students and their families, the tragedy of Fall 1981 will loom largest of all on the landscape of their Houghton story.

It was not until I arrived in Houghton as president that the impact of the eagles statue truly became part of my own Houghton story. Whenever there was an anniversary involving the class of 1982, the tragedy came to the fore. It was not only the students who remembered, but their families and friends. The re-living of the event was always gut-wrenching. But the painful grief was often made even more difficult by feelings that the college should have done more or should have done something differently. And then there are always the gnawing questions of "Where was God?" "Why wouldn't God intervene to spare such a talented group of Houghton students who could have done so much for the kingdom?" So it was not only the individual Houghton stories that were shaped by the event—but also the trajectories of lifetime journeys of faith.

The longer I was here, and the further we got from the fall of 1981, the more I realized that we needed to do more to keep the story alive for the students coming into Houghton who had not been here in 1981. It was important that the eagles monument not become just another campus marker given long ago with no immediate relevance to current students. It was staff in the alumni office who first suggested that we combine our "Welcome to Houghton" event held each fall for the entering class with the telling of the story of the eagles.

It was a brilliant idea. As we welcomed the class to become part of the Houghton community—gave them their purple and gold scarves and lit candles together—we also shared the story of the eagles, as they stood directly under the statue. We could have told it morbidly in a way that cast a pallor over the excitement and anticipation of the entering class. We could have told it melodramatically in a way that would have seemed surreal to the class—and left them confused about what they were supposed to feel.

Instead, we chose to narrate the story as descriptively as possible—trusting that the power of story would speak for itself. Then we sought to make three points—as relevant to the entering class as to those whose memory we sought to honor. First, we spoke of gratitude for the life of every student who comes to Houghton and how every student is a gift to those around them. Second, we spoke of the importance of choosing to live today in a way that is consistent with how we imagine we want to live our entire lives. It is so easy when we are young to think that someday "out there" we will make the kind of choices that we know we ought to make—and that, all told, we want to make when we are most honest with ourselves. Third, we spoke of the power of God's loving and redemptive improvisation to bring meaning and purpose out of the complex mix of pain and joy that is part of every one of our lives. And that, knowing this, we ought not to be afraid of all that lies ahead.[19]

FORTY YEARS OF GRIEVING

If grief has a timeline, it extends beyond forty years. Those who were close to The Six have now been carrying their grief longer than the children of Israel wandered through the wilderness, yet it remains. There doesn't seem to be an expiration date. The grief is different now—less intense, less debilitating, more intermittent—but still real and present. "I still think about them all the time." "Forty years later it still chokes me up." "I still feel it all these years later." "Over the years the pain has faded a bit, but it's still right there." "I still miss my brother every day."[20] Terry Anderson, Mark's brother, described his ongoing grief: "If I could have one prayer answered, it would be that my kids don't die before I do. It's easy to get inured to death, we see it on the front page of every paper, but every death is the loss of a parent or the loss of a child. It's devastating."[21]

Cindy Rudes' sister, Debbie, was washing dishes with Dawn dish soap when she received the phone call that changed her life, and to this day that smell still evokes the pain. "There isn't any Dawn in my house, I can tell you that."[22] Kevin Danielson, whose twenty-first birthday was the same day as the accident, describes it as "the saddest day of my life" and each ensuing birthday as a sobering reminder of the loss.[23] At the campus gathering on the night of the accident, the community sang the hymn, "It Is Well with My Soul." For some, the singing of that hymn still rekindles the grief of that night. The anniversary date of the accident, birthdays of the lost students, holidays, seeing the eagles sculpture on campus, the arrival of autumn, driving through or near the intersection in Wales, hearing about a car accident or other human tragedy—all these things and many others bring the occasionally dormant grief back to life. As one family member said: "Grief is never really finished. And every now and then, sometimes for no apparent reason, it comes out and slaps you across the face."[24] "Grieving never stops," remarked a classmate.[25]

The relentless wilderness of grieving is filled with questions about the unfulfilled futures of The Six. Speaking of his close friend Mark, classmate Glenn Burlingame said: "It's so hard to look at a life cut short, someone who had so much promise. What kind of person would he have become? What kind of parent would he have been? What kind of husband? What kind of lawyer? The loss of someone at that age—their whole future is gone. He was on the cusp of so much. The rest of us have lived all these years, lived different places, had jobs, had kids, and for Mark, none of that is there. That's the big, big hole."[26] Beth's sister Mindy reflected: "We had really high expectations for what the Lord was going to do with her in the future, and the hardest part for me was just seeing all that cut short."[27] Speaking of The Six, a staff member at the time said: "They had such potential. They were going places. I still wonder where they would be now. It seems like they could have done so much for the Lord."[28] None of The Six were able to ring any of the bells of adulthood. They didn't experience college graduation, marriage, parenting, meaningful careers, church leadership, grandchildren, retirement. Mark's brother Terry summarized his grief: "It's the sadness of what might have been."[29]

Standing shoulder to shoulder with the unanswerable questions about "what might have been" are the equally intractable questions about why. These are the questions of theodicy: the problem of reconciling the existence of a good God with the existence of suffering and evil. They are the questions of the ages, voiced by the psalmists, prophets, disciples, and church fathers. Even our Lord cried out in anguish from the cross: "My God, my God, why have you forsaken me?" (Matt. 27:46). In his memoir about the death of his twenty-five-year-old son in a mountain-climbing accident, Nicholas Wolterstoff wrote: "To the most agonized question I have ever asked I do not know the answer. I do not know why God would watch him fall. I do not know why God would watch me wounded. I cannot even guess."[30] Cindy Rudes' sister framed the question this way: "I know that my earthly father, Cindy's father, if he had the power to stop the truck, would have done it. So, if my earthly father would have done it, why didn't my Heavenly Father come through? Was he not paying attention?"[31]

Mike Walters said at the twenty-fifth anniversary service that these questions have "hung over the campus" since October 2, 1981—and it's clear that they have also hung over the lives of those who knew and loved The Six. Some felt so abandoned by God or found belief in a loving God so untenable that they walked away from the Christian faith altogether. Some entered lengthy seasons of doubt and disequilibrium and wrestling before coming back to faith later in life. Virtually everyone found that these questions required them to rethink much of what they believed about God. "It forced all these incredibly difficult questions on us. We hadn't had to grapple with death yet."[32] "I had to question what I thought I understood about faith. I didn't lose my faith, but my faith was so naïve at the time. We didn't have enough life experience to put something like that into perspective."[33] "I remember being very angry with God for a long time. I had lots of questions; it really challenged my faith."[34] "I don't think I doubted my faith at that point, but there were many years of coming back to that experience and mulling it over and trying to fit it into my theology. I had to reckon with the fact that bad things happen. It doesn't matter what your faith is, there are still horrible things that happen to good people."[35]

What is the outcome of four decades of wrestling with these questions? Have they arrived at any more clarity about the why? Some have found a degree of peace in their conviction that the accident was part of God's plan. "God has the plan in place. Sometimes he gives us people for only a short period of time."[36] "In God's wisdom, it was time to take them home."[37] "This was all in God's plan. Their lives have blessed so many other people, through their story and their Christian faith."[38] "I will never understand completely why God allowed the accident, but I firmly believe that his plans are perfect."[39] Others attribute the accident to the inevitable perils of living in a world that is governed by natural laws and fraught with risk and pain. "It's the sheer laws of physics—a smaller object gets hit by a larger object."[40] "I think God takes the bad events of life—caused by human error and/or the sinful world we live in—and uses them, but doesn't cause them. A truck, a wet day, someone not familiar with the road—a series of circumstances caused this."[41] "I don't believe God causes these things. In the beginning it was not part of God's plan—death, illness, accidents—these weren't the original plan. But we live now in a broken world."[42] "A fallen world couldn't ever be rendered accident-free."[43]

Many acknowledge the persistent elusiveness of meaningful and satisfactory answers. One alumnus who was close to The Six recalled how as a twenty-one-year-old, he couldn't figure out a way to make sense of the accident. He went on to say: "If you had asked me then, 'Will you have figured this out by the time you're sixty-four?' I would have said, 'Oh yeah, I'll have it figured out theologically and in every way.' And the thing is, I haven't. Forty years later, I still haven't found any place in my brain to put it, and it still doesn't make any sense to me. It began a lifelong struggle for me with the problem of sadness and evil and tragedy and cancer and accidents, and how you reconcile all that with God. I didn't have an answer then, and I don't know that I do now."[44] Others echo a similar sentiment: "My faith continues to be faith. I don't have answers that satisfy the whys of the tragedy."[45] "We won't know the whys on this side of heaven."[46] "I trust, but I still don't understand."[47] A sibling of one of The Six suggested the impossibility of an answer that would actually assuage the grief: "We don't know why, and there wouldn't be a good enough reason anyway. Even if God were to give an answer, it wouldn't be good enough to explain the death of my sister. There is no answer except that God is sovereign and that our highest act of praise is to trust him."[48]

Finding a way to continue trusting God—even when we don't understand, even when we walk with Job through unexplained and unfathomable suffering—is central to Christian faith. Annie Dillard wrote: "What is eternally fresh is our grief. What is eternally fresh is our astonishment. What is eternally fresh is our question: what in the Sam Hill is going on here? Is anyone running this show?"[49] How have people impacted by the accident learned to trust God in the face of their bewilderment about what happened? Some point to the mystery that is intrinsic to the attempt of finite humans to fathom an infinite God. "There are times when I wish I could cling to more certainty, so I go to the mystery of faith."[50] "God's ways are not our ways, so we have to reflect on God's character. He is good even when the bad and ugly is happening. It's a daily challenge to keep remembering and trusting in that."[51] "The accident was the most vivid illustration in my life of the fact that the Lord's understanding, no one can fathom."[52]

Others have found their faith bolstered by evidence that God is redeeming their suffering by bringing a measure of good out of it. Several of the siblings emphasized this idea. "The verse I stand on in all of this is Romans 8:28—that God can work all things together for good. God uses our mistakes, God uses our trauma, God has even used this accident for good."[53] "God, in his love and mercy, has transformed a horrible situation into something that has brought glory to him."[54] "God doesn't waste anything. In the economy of God, he can bring good out of every situation."[55] Another sibling described, with some reticence, a further dimension of her ability to trust in God: "Part of the healing process for me was, and I know this sounds heretical, but I had to forgive God for what he allowed to happen to my sister. I had to let him off the hook. I didn't want to, because I was still angry, still hurt. . . . But ten years after Cindy died, I was sitting on the sofa one day and I decided that I would believe that there is a God and that he does love me and that I was going to let it go. . . . Trust is a big one. It's a choice, not something I feel. It's the struggle between what I know to be true and what life feels like."[56]

In an article he wrote in the weeks following the accident, Dr. Chamberlain recalled how the hope of heaven was important to him in coming to terms with the accident: "They've simply been called to come home, I thought, for one moment reliving the short seconds when I heard my name paged over the airport public address system. . . . I knew Mark, Beth, Alan, Joy, Bert, and Cindy were celebrating a homecoming more festive than any we could have planned."[57] In an interview more than forty years after he wrote those words, Chamberlain reaffirmed the centrality of heaven in his framework for processing death: "As Christians, we have the hope of eternal life in heaven. We don't grieve like those with no hope. Those eagles on campus are to remind us that Christians don't look at death the way others do."[58] Kirsten Dyal Barton, the student who first told me about the accident as I walked to campus that Friday, reflected on the death of The Six and the death many years later of her own son: "Without the hope of heaven, we are lost. Tragic deaths like this remind us to cling to that hope."[59] A classmate described the hope of heaven as essential to coping with loss: "There HAS to be heaven! There has to be this reunion! Heaven has to be real, it has to be there, for us to be reunited with those we've lost."[60] Another remarked about the value of viewing time through the lens of eternity: "It [tragedy] prepares your heart for heaven, knowing that life in this world is a passing sliver in time and that what really counts is unseen."[61]

Some have pondered the implications of heavenly life for The Six. "For those of us who have lived these long lives, we would then be meeting someone who was twenty-two years old. Are they going to be twenty-two, and we'll be eighty-two? A life cut short is not a life we can really understand."[62] An editorial in the alumni magazine wondered similarly: "We find ourselves musing, sometimes, what it would be like to slip into heaven early. Our six friends never had to face September 11, arthritis, teenage children, and other trials that have etched wrinkles into our faces. What would it have been like to remain forever 20?"[63] A close friend of The Six who was nearly killed in a horrible car accident much later in life has wondered why she survived and they didn't. When asked if she thinks she was "protected" and The Six weren't, she remarked: "We think of protection from a purely earthly mindset. God sees eternity. Maybe those six are the protected or the blessed ones because they were spared the struggles of this life. I don't know. So many things I don't know. But I do know that I have this day to love and serve those around me and I hope to glorify God through it all." She then added another benefit of heavenly hope: "Won't it be wonderful to have eternity to ask these questions and to see clearly what we now muddle over?"[64]

While the hope of heaven is consistently identified as a great comfort in dealing with death, some also express caution about the ways in which placing immediate and undue emphasis on heaven can diminish the scope of the loss and impede the grieving process. One of Mark's close friends recalled, "When people said he's in a better place, my reaction was 'No, he's not. A better place would be sitting next to his girlfriend, Beth, not lying in a coffin.'" Reflecting on the value of the All Saints' Day practice in some Christian traditions of simply reading the names of the dead, he commented: "In the face of this kind of tragedy, even if you believe it has some sort of ultimate meaning, you can't say what that ultimate meaning is right when it happens. You're just lost and you're grieving—and you should be grieving, that's what it means to be human. The first thing you need to do is just acknowledge the loss and let people grieve. If your Christianity doesn't leave room for people to grieve, there's something wrong with your Christianity."[65]

Another friend of The Six remarked, "I felt a reassurance that even though they were gone from us physically, they're in a better place and they're OK—and that really helped. But I also think the hyper-spiritualizing got in the way of us being able to admit that we were really hurting and struggling and in shock. People were absolutely broken and shattered, but the narrative was all about spirituality and heaven. We could have used more counseling sessions, more dialogue, more small groups, more time in class to talk honestly about our feelings and our questions. I think we used our religious veneer to keep us from probing deeper issues."[66] Speaking of the prevailing narrative on campus about heaven and hope, another former student commented, "It was the only tool, the only vocabulary we had. I was in a dark place for a long time after the accident, so it became almost like performing. What was going on internally was very different from what I said when someone asked me about the accident. I felt like all I could do was roll out all the spiritual things I'd been trained to say at a time like that."[67]

The grief of Christians in the face of death, especially unexpected and premature death, is not a hopeless grief (1 Thess. 4:13), but it is grief, nonetheless.

Two friends of The Six who now work as counselors encourage great sensitivity to the crippling realities of that grief. Steve Jacobsen commented, "The platitudes don't acknowledge the complexities of grieving. When I grieve, I may feel many different things and some of them may be contradictory and sometimes all at the same time. The platitudes don't make loving space for the survivor to feel, express and ponder those complexities, including anger at an omnipotent God."[68] "Sometimes we sweep in with these victorious meanings that can inadvertently sweep people's suffering under the rug," said Jan Merz Kennedy.[69]

While no one would expect any Christian community to grieve perfectly, the presence of a community proved to be a healing balm. Mr. and Mrs. Anderson wrote, "In the blurred days after Mark died, we felt God's love for us, reflected through the love and support we received from the Houghton community. It was that sustaining love that helped carry us through the days and weeks following our loss. It meant so much to know that others were grieving with us over the loss of our son."[70] A schoolmate remembered, "Could we have done it better? No doubt. But I'm grateful for the community of Houghton to walk it all through with. It was a truly caring community."[71] Another remarked, "Sometimes the grief can be so deep and profound that we need others to sob for us, because it hurts too much to mourn all the time."[72] Pastor Mark Abbott reflected recently: "I was a lead pastor for forty-two years in three different churches and am now in my seventies. There has been no tragedy in my experience that has been so gripping and so seared my own heart as did the Houghton tragedy of 1981. And nowhere have I so experienced a faith community sharing its grief together and in the presence of the God who shares our grief."[73]

Those impacted by profound grief have found meaning in their heightened awareness of the brevity and preciousness of life. Beth Andes' sister reflected on her family's experience: "We walked away with a deep understanding that none of us knows how long we will have. God understands the number of our days, but we don't. And it's a reality check—how am I serving God today? None of us know how long we're going to be here, and we just need to treasure every day, and value what God wants to do through us each day."[74] Speaking of his six lost friends, Graham Drake mused, "I think from time to time of what they could have been at this point in their lives, and if I am living up to my potential by mysteriously continuing to survive. We don't know the reasons why, but that can be sort of a reminder that life is contingent and risky, and what are you doing today? I still think about it, and it still matters."[75] A classmate who lives in the Buffalo area and regularly drives through the intersection commented, "I often think about the fact that as they approached it that day they had no idea they were seconds away from their eternal home. We have no assurances in this life of another hour or another day and need to live with making the most of the days we have."[76] Said another: "God has given me this life and I am grateful for it. Every day is a gift."[77]

Scripture provides numerous images that poke through our illusions about the permanence of our earthly lives: our lives are like grass, a flower, a mist. Beautiful and precious, but fragile and fleeting. We are foolish if we take the future for granted. Those who lived through October 2, 1981, encountered that reality in an excruciating fashion and now seek to live the one and only life they have with the enriched understanding sought by the psalmist: "Teach us to number our days, that we may gain a heart of wisdom" (Ps. 90:12). It's the wisdom that sees every day, each tick of the clock, every breath we take, and every morning we wake up as gifts from God.

Those who live with this deep gratitude for each day often describe an equally deep love for the people God has given with whom they are able to enjoy each day. If the accident taught the community one thing, it may have been that people are sacred and that our relationships with them are priceless. Looking back on the last forty years, friends and family speak with clarity and passion about their intense commitment to cherish the people they love. "The accident helped me become much more thankful in the moment for time with friends. Any of them could be taken at any time and you never know when that might happen, so be thankful for any time you have with people."[78] "I make sure I say 'I love you' to my kids and close friends every time I say good-bye. You need to make sure things are right with people, that they know how much you care, because you never know."[79] Speaking of those who knew The Six, a classmate said, "I'm guessing we probably all take our time with every goodbye. We might think of them when we commit to resolving a quarrel as soon as possible."[80]

The grief of one of the parents was multiplied many times over because of an unresolved conflict between parent and child at the time of the accident.

The realization that the issue could now never be resolved was traumatic for the parent and illustrated for the family the critical importance of keeping relationships current and always nurturing love.[81] Twenty-five years after the accident, Mr. and Mrs. Anderson reflected on the centrality of love in their own lives: "Twenty-five years ago we received the shattering news that our son, Mark, had been killed in an automobile accident. After twenty-five years, our memories of Mark have begun to fade and the intensity of our pain has receded. So, what has remained? The love. Our love for our son; our son's love for his family, friends, and the truth; and the love we felt from his friends, classmates, and God. . . . Although so many years have passed, what remains is what sustains us: our love for Mark, the love the Houghton community had for Mark and us in our loss; Mark's love for his family, friends, and God; and God's love and support of us."[82] Their words contain the echoes of the apostle Paul: "Love never fails" (1 Cor. 13:8).

Many seek to make sense of the accident by pointing to various ways in which good has come out of it. The words of three members of the class of 1982 illustrate this sentiment: "Until we reach eternity, we will never really know the total impact of the accident on our campus, community, and world. The never-ending ripple of that we will never know." "I often think about the far-reaching tentacles of all the people who were impacted by this." "Only eternity will reveal all of the good that came from such a tragic event."[83] Their words reflect the confidence of Romans 8:28 mentioned earlier: that God can redeem even the worst of tragedy by bringing some sort of good out of it.

What are these good things that people point to? Some trace their sense of calling to vocational ministry back to the aftermath of the accident. A few hours after Al Bushart's funeral, his classmate Tedd Smith found himself so overwhelmed with the weight of the loss that he pulled his car off the side of the road and broke down weeping over the steering wheel. Before long, however, he found himself reflecting on the Christ-centered lives of The Six and the hope of heaven and began to feel a deep sense of peace. He said these words out loud in his car: "Lord, if I can have peace like this in a time like this, then you're the one I want to serve for the rest of my life in whatever form you want." Tedd had been planning on a lucrative business career and instead gave his entire career to a parachurch ministry for teenagers and a local church pastorate. "Some might say it was just the emotion of the moment, but I've lived out this calling for forty-plus years now," he said, "and I can go back to a confidence that the Lord called me into ministry through a tragic event. That call still sustains me; it was a keystone moment in my life. There is hope and peace available to us even in the midst of the deepest pain."[84] Missionaries Brian and Chris Davidson point to the "huge impact" the loss of their close friends had in their lives: "so much so that we realized tomorrow isn't promised to us, and it was a fuel to our passion for missions."[85] The accident prompted Barbara Isaman Bushart to embark on a quest to understand human suffering more fully, which eventually led her into pastoral ministry.[86]

Others point to ways in which the trauma of the accident gave them tools for ministry to others. Jeff Jordan has worked in higher education student development his entire career, including many crisis situations that involved campus tragedy and student death. "The 1981 accident didn't 'prepare' me for any of these; I don't think you can 'be prepared' for tragic situations since each one is so unique. But one does come to understand that in these situations there are ways to react and respond, in the moment and after the event."[87] Jan Merz Kennedy, whose career has been in pastoral care and counseling, said, "I felt like I graduated from Houghton with a minor in death, and that close and intimate experience with death has helped me deal with suffering and human adversity."[88] Cindy Rudes' sister, Debbie, reflected on how her own loss has helped her support others in their times of grief: "They know I can begin to understand their grief because of my own grief. They can talk to me. They tell me I'm safe—that I don't judge them for their questions and struggles."[89] In the later years of their lives, Al Bushart's parents started a chapter of Compassionate Friends, an organization that supports parents who have lost children.[90] Their grief enabled them to become, as Henri Nouwen suggested, "wounded healers."[91]

The family of Bert Rapp turned their grief into generosity. Almost immediately after the accident, they established the Bert Rapp Scholarship at Houghton to assist needy students with the costs of their Houghton education. Several dozen students have benefited from the generous scholarships available through this endowed fund. Tanya Shire, who served as women's volleyball coach during Joy and Cindy's freshman, sophomore, and junior years, recently established the Joy Ellis and Cynthia Rudes Women's Volleyball Endowment which provides funds to supplement the women's volleyball program. And as President Chamberlain announced in the days immediately after the accident, the college established an endowed scholarship fund in memory of all six students. Many donors have contributed to what is now called the Soaring Eagles Scholarship, which is awarded to students (typically juniors) who require extra financial assistance to complete their studies at Houghton.[92]

Many friends and family members speak of the accident as a painful but effective catalyst for their own spiritual and personal growth. They speak of character development in such areas as more gentleness and patience with others, more gratitude for life, more motivation to seize opportunities, more thoughtfulness in approaching Scripture, more reliance on God's strength, more acceptance of life's mysteries, more sober mindedness about the consequences of decisions. As classmate Martha Manikas-Foster summarized, "The death of The Six changed my life. I'm not alone. It's worked its way into each of us in its own way."[93]

The intersection of Routes 78 and 20A in the Town of Wales remains a silent witness to the events of October 2, 1981. A classmate of The Six who has driven there many times over the years said: "Every drive past that house, the gas station, and the intersection has been a silent one. Our children, even when young, knew this was a piece of roadway where we stayed quiet."[94] In response to the outcry after the accident, the intersection was eventually redesigned to make it safer. Route 78 north, the road on which The Six were traveling, has been rerouted to the east and straightened so that its intersection with Route 20A is no longer a gentle, sweeping curve; it now approaches at close to a 90-degree angle, making the crossroads much more apparent. The stop sign on Route 78 north has been supplemented with a flashing red traffic light. Those driving east or west on Route 20A now see a yellow flashing light at the intersection, and their speed limit has been reduced to a more reasonable 45 miles per hour.

Looking west from the "new" intersection, one can still see the long hill down which Mr. Bingenheimer was driving in the moments before the crash. He died on May 17, 2019, at the age of eighty-eight, and was survived by his wife of sixty-eight years, Joan, and their four children. A fifty-one-year-old man at the time of the accident, he lived thirty-seven more years afterward. We can only imagine how the second half of his life must have been shaped and scarred by what transpired at the bottom of the hill, and how the compassion of the Houghton community may have brought some grace. Looking across Route 20A to the northwest, the house where Mr. Kohn was hanging his flowers on that Friday morning still stands. In front is the narrow yard that slopes up from the roadway, across which the crumpled Dasher was pushed by the tractor trailer. A large tree towers over the yard, perhaps marking the very spot where the car came to rest. The Six have now been gone more than twice as long as they had been alive prior to that moment.

And at the southwest corner of the intersection, across the road from Mr. Kohn's house, one can still see the path of the original Route 78 where The Six spent their last seconds alive. Now called Old Strykersville Road, it is a rarely used side street about 250 yards long that provides access to four homes and ends at a small circular turnaround. The man who lives in the home next to the turnaround remarked: "I was six years old when it happened, but I'll never forget that day."[95] Standing in that gravel turnaround, one can clearly see the path taken by the blue Dasher, the location of the stop sign that was missed, the direction from which the tractor trailer was coming, and the spot in the roadway where the collision occurred: the collision of a truck and a car, the collision of one man and six college students, the collision of life and death, the collision of heaven and earth, the collision of a split second and eternity.

Thirty-eight miles to the southeast six eagles spread their wings and soar.

TEARS IN A BOTTLE

The story I wanted to tell is complete. I offer this personal postscript only because, when I read a story, I find it helpful to understand the vantage point from which the author is telling the story. No researcher or author is completely objective; our biases, viewpoints, and experiences inevitably influence what we see, how we interpret what we see, and how we share what we've seen. If someone else had written this book, it would have been a different book. So, I think it is only fair to you to tell you briefly how the events of October 2, 1981, impacted me personally so you can know the backstory that inevitably shaped the story told in this book.

In the days immediately after the accident, like many of my schoolmates, my response was one of deepened spiritual fervor. The only framework I had for trying to understand and respond to the accident was the Christian faith of my childhood and teenage years. So I began praying with more intensity and reading the Bible with more regularity and paying attention in chapel with more intentionality. I even started attending our class prayer meeting on Tuesday nights, which I had never done prior to October 2. I was inspired by the stories that were being told around campus of the devotion of The Six and stirred by the ways in which the entire campus seemed to respond with confidence in God. My own rather pedestrian spiritual life seemed tepid in comparison and inadequate for what had transpired, and so I began seeking God with new passion.

A couple weeks after the accident, I asked my pastor father if I could share in church how God was using the accident to bring renewed spiritual vitality to the campus and to my own life. Unbeknownst to me, my mother saved my notes from that talk and recently dug them out for me. I wish she hadn't. The banality of my title—"Elmira Wesleyan Church, October 18, 1981"—is matched by the simplicity and naivete of what I said. "God is turning this accident into a good thing! Our earthly lives are worthless! Don't waste your time on anything other than God!" I was one week shy of my twentieth birthday so I suppose I can be forgiven for enthusiasm that outstripped my wisdom and sensitivity. But that talk provides a window into the state of my soul in the days immediately following the accident. Committed. Zealous. Passionate. Eager. Hopeful.

It didn't last.

As fall turned into winter, a wintry spirit began to overtake my soul. As the spiritual and emotional intensity of the accident's immediate aftermath began to fade, as I began to sit with the enormity of what had happened, as I began to ask questions for which there did not seem to be any answers, I entered a season of my life that can best be described with words that often characterize an upstate New York winter. Barren. Cold. Bleak. Empty. Desolate.

I had been introduced to the problem of evil as a concept in a philosophy class taught by one of the gurus of the Houghton faculty in the 1980s, Dr. Brian Sayers. If God exists, and if God is completely loving and all-powerful, then why do evil and suffering exist in this world that God has made? If God wants to prevent suffering but is not able to do so, then God must not be all-powerful. If God can prevent suffering but chooses not to, then God must not be completely loving. Since evil and suffering are so prevalent in our world, then either God is not all-loving, is not all-powerful, or does not exist at all. I imagine I took diligent notes in philosophy class that day and thought the problem of evil was an interesting intellectual conundrum, but then gave it little further thought as I rushed off to a meal or an intramural basketball game.

But the accident of October 2 turned the general problem of evil into a particular, personal problem for me. I was asking all the same questions almost everyone else seemed to be asking: How could God have allowed this to happen? How hard would it have been for God to delay for one second (one second!) the arrival of the car or the truck at that intersection? Why didn't God prompt Mark Anderson or Mr. Bingenheimer to take a different route? Why didn't God clear the rain away? If God can create the universe and part the Red Sea and raise people from the dead, why didn't God reach a little pinky finger down from heaven and do something simple to prevent this horrific accident from happening? Maybe he isn't as good as I'd been taught. Or as powerful as the Bible stories suggested. Or maybe he isn't there at all.

Stress cracks began to penetrate the foundations of my faith. I began to question everything I'd ever believed about God. I remember going to the college library one evening and perusing the world religions section of the stacks, looking for a religion that made more sense to me. I signed up for a class on existentialism, not out of noble intellectual curiosity, but because that's what I figured I'd become. Or at least it sounded sophisticated to say, "I'm an existentialist." I pestered faculty members like Dr. Bressler, Dr. Sayers, and Dr. Schultz with questions about how they could believe in a God who allowed horrible things to happen. I began to listen cynically to prayers about help with homework or girlfriend problems or financial needs ("You really think God is going to help you with something trivial like that when he couldn't be bothered to stop six of our friends from being killed?"). One evening, when I was lying in bed staring at the ceiling, turning all these questions over in my mind, I overheard two of my housemates discussing how concerned they were about me. Their concern was justified; the faith I had known my entire life was slipping through my fingers. I could not find a way to reconcile what I had always believed to be true about God with what had happened in the Town of Wales on that rainy Friday morning.

By the end of the 1981–82 school year, I began to think of myself as an agnostic. My plans for life after Houghton switched from theological seminary and pastoral ministry to climbing the corporate ladder. I might as well get rich, I thought. As was the campus tradition, I continued to bow my head and close my eyes before meals in the campus center—but now instead of thanking a good God for my food, I spent those moments wondering how my friends could possibly still believe in that God. I could still trot out the pious-sounding clichés when I needed to, but I was merely playing a role. One of my senior-year classes required each student to lead a brief Bible study for the class; I remember fulfilling the assignment while thinking, "I don't believe a word of this anymore." Our commencement speaker was the noted Christian apologist Charles Colson, and his brilliant speech gave me a glimmer of hope that the Christian faith might be reasonable—but I was nowhere near ready to endorse that viewpoint. I drove off the Houghton campus after graduation with a wonderful education and a cherished group of lifelong friends, but a faith that had not survived the accident. I doubted I would ever return.

My journey back to faith was a long and bumpy one. A beloved grandmother died, and once again I was confronted up close and personal with the realities of life and death. Despite the nice salary and the European sports car I had my eyes on, the dream job I had landed in corporate America turned out to be utterly unsatisfying. While my new business colleagues spent their free time finding creative ways to blow all the money we were making, I was reading books about the problem of evil and world religions and trying to make sense of the universe. I wasn't much fun at parties. I lived in Buffalo at the time, about twenty minutes from the site of the accident, and on weekends, drove quite regularly to the intersection in the Town of Wales to ponder what had happened there.

The conversations I'd had with Houghton faculty members during my junior and senior year continued to roll around in my mind. Dr. Sayers, the brilliant philosopher, had helped me see the limits of logic and rationality— that a leap of faith was involved in believing almost anything and that questions and doubts were normal. Dr. Schultz, the Old Testament scholar, described for me how the Christian conception of God involves one who willingly entered our suffering world, died the most painful and unfair of deaths imaginable, and so shares in our suffering. My English professor and friend, Dr. Bressler, introduced me to the writings of G. K. Chesterton who helped me imagine a God who is much larger, more mysterious, and more inscrutable than my Sunday school conceptions of God had been.

I continued to marvel at the deep piety and compassion I'd seen lived out before me by the six lost students, their closest friends, and the Houghton community. I wondered how the world and everything in it—the good, the beautiful, the painful, the inexplicable—could have somehow sprung from some sort of cosmic accident. I remained intrigued and moved by the tender compassion of Jesus Christ. Finally, with a wavering faith that contained more questions than answers, more doubts than certainties, and more tentativeness than confidence, I chose to believe again in the existence of a good, loving, all-powerful God who came to us in the person of Jesus Christ. If you had asked me in that moment why I did it, I probably would have echoed the words of the apostle Peter—"To whom [else] shall we go?" (John 6:68). Peter didn't see a lot of other good options outside of trusting in Christ, and neither did I. I'd gone to the library and looked.

Forty years have passed since I took that faltering step of faith. Although I graduated from seminary (twice), married a wonderful Christian woman I met at Houghton, raised a family, and served in vocational Christian ministry for thirty-five years, I still struggle with many of the questions that emerged from the accident. My wife has suggested that my life verse should be "Lord, I believe; help my unbelief" (Mark 9:24 NKJV), and I think she's right. My bookshelves sag with titles like *Disappointment with God*, *The Problem of Pain*, *Faith & Doubt*, *The Gospel of Coincidence*, *Where Is God When It Hurts*?, and *Learning to Walk in the Dark*. Even "Why I Am Not a Christian," a lecture by the famous atheist Bertrand Russell, has a spot. A look back over twenty-five years of sermon titles reveals that I often inflicted upon congregations the questions with which I continued to struggle: "The Upside of Doubt," "When God Is Silent," "Why Is There So Much Evil in the World?" and "Making Sense of Suffering."

To this day, I struggle when Christians talk with certainty about how God protected them or intervened for them during some sort of problem or calamity (Why didn't God protect The Six? Are you sure you weren't just lucky?). I struggle when people pray for safe travel (Wouldn't the parents of The Six have prayed that prayer for their children countless times?), good parking spaces (Really? God will help you park but wouldn't help those students survive?), or nice weather for the church picnic (Can I tell you about a time when nice weather might have saved six lives?). I react viscerally when people throw off the Christian cliché: "God is in control." (Always? Can I tell you about a day when I don't think he was? Or at least I hope he wasn't?) The problem of evil is still vexing for me. While I think the existence of anything at all is a huge problem for atheists, I also think the fact that so much of what exists is a mess is a huge problem for Christian theists. I am so sympathetic to those who have genuine, well-reasoned doubts about faith—especially those who have suffered—that I'm uneasy asserting with confidence the usual formulas about who goes to heaven and who doesn't make it. I hope the wideness in God's mercy is wide enough for those, like me, who doubt.

Pastor Mark Abbott, who was referenced in this story and was my college pastor, used to talk in sermons about a "question box" where we can put all the questions we have for God. I can remember him saying with some regularity, "That will have to go in my question box." My question box seems to get larger and fuller with every passing year, and the questions seem to get more complicated. I think most will remain unanswered this side of eternity. Most days, my faith is no bigger than a mustard seed. Like Jacob, I wrestle with God and walk with a limp. The aftershocks of October 2, 1981, continue to vibrate in my mind and soul.

You have already heard a number of voices more eloquent than my own describe how they have tried to make sense of it all. I cannot improve upon what they have said. Let me instead simply name for you three ideas, all mentioned in their words, that I return to time and again and that bring solace to my life and faith.

First, I have come to see questions and doubts not as some sort of problem with faith, but as intrinsic to the nature of faith. Faith is only required, after all, when we have doubts. When we know something with certainty, what role does faith even play anymore? Any thorough reading of Scripture suggests that God leaves plenty of room for the honest asking of hard questions, the acknowledgment of uncertainty, the deep questions of the soul, the struggle with life's messiness. The psalmist's entreaty of the Lord is fairly typical: "Awake, Lord! Why do you sleep? Rouse yourself! Do not reject us forever. Why do you hide your face and forget our misery and oppression?" (Ps. 44:23–24). The biblical stories of Job, Habakkuk, John the Baptist, Abraham and Sarah, Job, the writers of the Psalms of Lament, Thomas, the post-Easter doubters, and so many more include piercing questions and heartfelt doubts. Even Jesus on the cross, in his full experience of the frailty and suffering of the human condition, wondered why. I struggle with versions of Christianity that see this sort of wrestling as somehow deficient.

The efforts of the human mind to fully apprehend the mysteries of God and faith and life will always come up light years short, and so we are left inevitably with question boxes that overflow. I think God understands. In his sermon at the twenty-fifth anniversary service, Mike Walters shared the words of Thomas Merton: "Can I tell you that I have found answers to the questions that torment a man of our time? I do not know if I have found answers. God is a being to be known, not a problem to be solved. One cannot know God as long as he attempts to solve the problem of God."[1]

Second, I have come to rely more deeply on the faith of the Christian community as a scaffolding for my own. The first sermon I ever preached was at a family reunion at our church camp not far from the Houghton campus. I was a young seminary student, only a couple years removed from my post-accident years of agnosticism, and someone in my extended family courageously decided to let me attempt a sermon at our Sunday morning "service." The text I selected was the account of Jesus healing a paralyzed man who was carried to him on a mat by some other men. Matthew, Mark, and Luke all tell the story and include the rather surprising news that Jesus healed the paralyzed man "when he saw *their* faith" (my emphasis; Matt. 9:2; Mark 2:5; Luke 5:20). The paralytic was healed not because of his own faith, but because of the faith of those who brought him. It isn't even clear that the paralytic had any faith at all of his own. I don't have my notes from that sermon anymore (perhaps my mother does), but I remember talking about the fact that those of us with little or weak faith (thinking of myself, of course) can receive Christ's grace by virtue of the greater faith of those around us.

Forty years after that sermon, I rely even more completely on the faith of those around me to bolster my own. My wife's earnest prayers each morning for our children; the gathered church standing to declare in one voice, "I believe in God the Father Almighty, maker of heaven and earth," and then gathering around a simple table to eat bread and drink from a cup; my friends and colleagues who serve the Lord and love me so faithfully; Houghton classmates who at our reunion ponder forty years of God's faithfulness; the communion of saints throughout history and around the world. Perhaps the greatest blessing of working on this book for me has been the opportunity to hear about and be strengthened by the faith of the family members and friends of those who were lost on October 2. They don't have answers either. None of us do. But their tenacious clinging to God amid their suffering is an example and encouragement to me; they are now part of the "great cloud of witnesses" that inspire me to run my own race with perseverance (Heb. 12:1).

Barbara Brown Taylor writes about those who experience "full solar spirituality," which includes such benefits as "a sure sense of God's presence, certainty of belief, divine guidance in all things, and reliable answers to prayer."[2] She describes her own experience of God as more of a "lunar spirituality," which includes seasons of darkness, feelings of divine absence, unanswered prayer, questions about faith, and "doubts about the health of my soul."[3] I often wish my faith was full solar, and perhaps there are steps I should have taken that would have turned up the lights. But my more lunar spirituality leaves me in the enviable position of being able to lean more frequently and more heavily on the faith of the church. My "personal" relationship with Christ is not very personal at all; it is utterly interconnected with the faith of others—the corporate body of Christ.

Finally, I have continued to find hope and meaning in the idea about God that was first shared with me by Houghton professor Carl Schultz in the months after the accident—that God may not give us a perfect answer to our suffering, but in Christ, he has entered our suffering world and shares our sufferings with us. I have often turned to the way two great authors have articulated this truth. First, Dorothy Sayers: "For whatever reason God chose to make man as he is— limited and suffering and subject to sorrow and death—He had the honesty and courage to take His own medicine. Whatever game He is playing with His creation, He has kept His own rules and played fair. He can exact nothing from man that He has not exacted from Himself."[4] And Nicholas Wolterstorff, who wrote about the accidental death of his young adult son: "Through the prism of my tears I have seen a suffering God. It is said of God that no one can behold his face and live. I always thought this meant that no one could see his splendor and live. A friend said perhaps it meant that no one could see his sorrow and live. Or perhaps his sorrow is his splendor."[5]

Perhaps no image of God sharing in our suffering is more beautiful than the one provided by the psalmist: "You keep track of all my sorrows. You have collected all my tears in your bottle" (Ps. 56:8 NLT). This has been a story of tears. The tears of the first responders. The tears of Sheriff Braun at the birthday luncheon after he left the accident scene. The tears of moms and dads and brothers and sisters as they received the news that changed their lives. The tears of a campus community. The tears of six funerals and six gravesides. The tears of a college president. The tears that have been shed around kitchen tables and Christmas trees and six soaring eagles for more than forty years and counting. Tears that have fallen like the raindrops of that Friday morning in Wales Center and flowed like the mighty Niagara not far away. Your tears and mine. Past tears, present tears, and future tears.

We still don't know why the suffering that brought the tears came, but we have this assurance about all those tears: that God sees them and collects them all in his bottle. Our tears don't go unnoticed. Our tears aren't forgotten or ignored or dismissed. They matter to God and are treasured by him. And they will continue to be cherished until that great day when our faith will be sight, when our homecoming will be eternal, and when all our tears will be wiped away by the Man of Sorrows, our suffering Savior, the Jesus who wept. I imagine his eyes, too, will be glistening as well.

ENDNOTES

THE SIX

1. Daniel Chamberlain and Evelyn Bence, "The Homecoming," *Christian Herald,* October 1982, 28.
2. All information about Mark Anderson's pre-Houghton years is from author interviews with Mark's brothers Keith Anderson (October 3, 2023) and Terry Anderson (October 5, 2023).
3. *"mortar between the bricks"*: Terry Anderson interview with author (October 5, 2023); *"oil in the engine"*: Keith Anderson interview with author (October 3, 2023).
4. Houghton College, "Memorialized Students' Biographies," press release, October 8, 1981. Houghton University Archives.
5. Houghton College, "Personal data form" for Mark Anderson, September 1981, Houghton University Archives.
6. Susan Facer, personal correspondence to Mr. and Mrs. Bert Anderson, October 18, 1982.
7. Houghton College, "Memorialized Students' Biographies."
8. Terry Anderson, interview with author, October 5, 2023.
9. Houghton College, "Memorialized Students' Biographies."
10. Bill Doezema, in focus group discussion with author, November 13, 2023.
11. *"great mind"*: Tedd Smith, interview with author, October 26, 2023; *"super-smart"*: Jon Horton, email message to author, October 2023; *"powerful, often overwhelming intellect"*: Rich Hawkins, personal correspondence to Mr. and Mrs. Bert Anderson, May 6, 1982.
12. Jeff Jordan, email message to author, September 21, 2023.
13. Glenn Burlingame, interview with author, December 3, 2023.
14. Burlingame, interview.
15. Hawkins, correspondence.
16. Author's personal recollection.
17. Terry Anderson, interview.
18. Mark Anderson, "Maintaining Open Forum," *Houghton Star*, September 18, 1981.
19. The script from this undated speech, in Mark's handwriting, was provided to the author by the Anderson family.
20. Tim Nichols, interview with the author, October 12, 2023.
21. *"extremely serious about Christianity"*: Hawkins, correspondence.
22. Bert and Doris Anderson, personal correspondence, 2006.

23. Mark Anderson, journal entry, May 24, 1981.

24. Hawkins, correspondence.

25. Hawkins, correspondence.

26. Terry Anderson, interview.

27. Terry Anderson, interview.

28. Terry Anderson, interview.

29. Burlingame, interview.

30. Burlingame, interview.

31. Mark Anderson, journal entry, May 24, 1981.

32. All information about Beth Andes' pre-Houghton years is from the author's interview with her sister, Mindy Andes (January 21, 2024).

33. Andes, interview.

34. Andes, interview.

35. Andes, interview.

36. Mercy Zecher Dawson, email messages to author, January–February, 2024.

37. Zecher Dawson, email.

38. Houghton College, "Personal data form" for Beth Andes, September 1981, Houghton University Archives.

39. Sara Solovitch, "Homecoming Plans Led to Fatal Journey," *Buffalo Courier Express*, October 3, 1981.

40. Zecher Dawson, email.

41. Mercy Zecher, "Beth R. Andes," *Houghton Star*, October 9, 1981.

42. "Tragedy, Triumph and the Ultimate Homecoming," *Houghton Milieu*, November 1981.

43. Nichols, interview.

44. Zecher, "Beth R. Andes," *Houghton Star*.

45. Zecher Dawson, email.

46. Zecher, "Beth R. Andes," *Houghton Star*.

47. Assisi prayer quoted in Zecher, "Beth R. Andes," *Houghton Star*.

48. Andes, interview.

49. Joan Dickenson, "Houghton Students Extol Spirit of 6 Crash Victims," *Buffalo Courier Express*, October 11, 1981.

50. Except where specifically noted, information about Alan Bushart's pre-Houghton years comes from an interview with Warren and Barbara Bushart (November 13, 2016) and email correspondence from Kevin Bushart to the author (December 2016).

51. *a little dickens*: "Words of Comfort," *Rochester Democrat & Chronicle*, October 4, 1981.

52. *didn't turn into an angel*: Barbara Bushart, interview with author, November 13, 2016.

53. "Words of Comfort," *Rochester Democrat & Chronicle*, October 4, 1981.

54. Barbara Bushart, interview with author, November 13, 2016.

55. Connie Finney, interview with author, October 30, 2023.

56. Doug Burke, quoted in the *Houghton Star*, October 9, 1981.

57. Doug Burke, interview with author, February 2, 2024.

58. Brian Davidson, remarks at Houghton University athletic event attended by author, October 21, 2023.

59. Several people made this observation: Dexter Davis (interview with author, September 26, 2023), Jeff Jordan (email message to author, September 21, 2023), and Doug Roorbach (email message to author, November 2023).
60. Jeff Jordan, email message to author, September 21, 2023.
61. Davidson, Houghton University athletic event.
62. John Irwin, *Houghton Star*, October 9, 1981.
63. Bob Chiapperino, *Houghton Star*, October 9, 1981.
64. Jon Ortlip, *Houghton Star*, October 9, 1981.
65. Barbara Bushart, interview with author, November 13, 2016.
66. Barbara Bushart, interview.
67. Warren Bushart, interview with author, November 13, 2016.
68. Kathie Brenneman, interview with author, October 2016.
69. James Mullen, in focus group discussion with author, November 13, 2023.
70. Nichols, interview.
71. Warren Bushart, interview.
72. Steve Jacobsen, email messages to author, February–March 2024.
73. Doug Burke, quoted in the *Houghton Star*, October 9, 1981.
74. Warren and Barbara Bushart, interview.
75. "Words of Comfort" *Rochester Democrat & Chronicle,* October 4, 1981.
76. This story was told by Dr. Daniel Chamberlain at the campus memorial service on October 7, 1981, and shared with the author by Dr. Robert Danner on September 1, 2016.
77. "A Joy Forever," 2021, 22. Houghton University Archives.
78. "Former Genevan Among 6 Killed," *Finger Lakes Times*, October 3, 1981.
79. "Joy Forever," 22.
80. Houghton College, "Personal data form" for Joy Ellis, September 1981, Houghton University Archives.
81. "Joy Forever," 24.
82. Marsha Davis, "Those Who Knew Her Recall Victim as 'Joy,'" *Watertown Daily Times*, October 3, 1981.
83. Davis, "Those Who Knew Her."
84. Davis, "Those Who Knew Her."
85. "Former Genevan," *Finger Lakes Times*.
86. Janet Carlson Tennies, email message to author, December 3, 2016.
87. Keith Epstein, "The Ripples Cast by an 'Ordinary' Life," *Watertown Daily Times*, October 13, 1981.
88. Tanya Shire Hildebrandt, interview with author, October 27, 2023.
89. "Tragedy, Triumph," *Houghton Milieu*.
90. Phil Stockin, in focus group discussion with author, November 13, 2023.
91. Tedd Smith, interview with author, October 6, 2023.
92. Epstein, "Ripples."
93. Houghton College, "Personal data form" for Joy Ellis.
94. Richard "Jake" Jacobsen, interview with author, February 8, 2017.
95. Epstein, "Ripples."
96. *"led with a smile"*: Steve Jacobsen, email message to author, March 1, 2024; *"always saw the good things"*: Davis, "Those Who Knew Her"; *"always bubbly"*: Betty Bowser Young, interview with author, November 22, 2023.

97. David Frazier, interview with author, October 3, 2023.

98. "Jake" Jacobsen, interview.

99. Marlene Gifford, interview with author, October 24, 2023.

100. Epstein, "Ripples."

101. Chris Schmitt Davidson, remarks at Houghton University athletic event attended by author, October 21, 2023.

102. Mary Beth Fuller Bowling, interview with author, November 13, 2023.

103. Keith Epstein, "Six 'Live' in Friends' Hearts," *Watertown Daily Times*, October 8, 1981.

104. Jan Merz Kennedy, interview with author, October 6, 2023.

105. Janet Franz Nelson, email message to author, November 28, 2016.

106. Epstein, "Ripples."

107. Epstein, "Ripples."

108. Gifford, interview.

109. Schmitt Davidson, Houghton University athletic event.

110. Epstein, "Ripples."

111. This observation was made by several people, including Marlene Gifford (interview with author, October 24, 2023), Betsy Lundell Carosa (interview with author, January 4, 2024) and Ruth Hutton in her article "The Ultimate Homecoming" (*Moody Monthly*, March 1982).

112. Rob Jacobsen, interview with author, November 13, 2023.

113. Solovitch, "Homecoming Plans."

114. Ed Taylor, interview with author, October 12, 2023.

115. Houghton College, "Personal data form" for Bert Rapp, September 1981, Houghton University Archives.

116. Houghton College, "Memorialized Students' Biographies."

117. Rob Ruth, interview with author, November 8, 2023.

118. Gifford, interview.

119. Jon Bradley, social media message to author, October 21, 2023.

120. Author's personal recollection.

121. Ruth, interview.

122. Nichols, interview.

123. Taylor, interview.

124. Graham Drake, interview with author, November 8, 2023.

125. Frazier, interview.

126. "Tragedy, Triumph," *Houghton Milieu*.

127. Ruth, interview.

128. Taylor, interview.

129. Ruth, interview.

130. Karyn Hecht, email message to author, March 22, 2024.

131. Steve Dunbar, email message to author, November 2016.

132. Rob Jacobsen, interview.

133. Dunbar, email.

134. Frazier, interview.

135. Taylor, interview.

136. Taylor, interview.

137. Solovitch, "Homecoming Plans."

138. Hecht, email.

139. Ruth Hutton, "The Ultimate Homecoming," *Moody Monthly*, March 1982, 137.

140. Ruth, interview.

141. Austin Swallow, "Albert L. Rapp," *Houghton Star*, October 9, 1981.

142. *"on a great path"*: David Frazier (interview with author, October 3, 2023); *"success at anything"*: Steve Dunbar (email message to author, November 2016).

143. Barry Conboy, Hudson City Savings Bank, letter to Houghton College, October 5, 1981. Houghton University Archives.

144. Dunbar, email.

145. Ruth, interview.

146. All information about Cindy Rudes' pre-Houghton years is from an author interview with Cindy's sister, Debbie Rudes Haas, October 3, 2023.

147. Betty Bowser, "Cynthia R. Rudes," *Houghton Star*, October 9, 1981.

148. Bowser, "Cynthia R. Rudes," *Houghton Star*.

149. Hutton, "Ultimate Homecoming," 135.

150. Betty Bowser Young, interview with author, November 22, 2023.

151. Gifford, interview.

152. Gifford, interview.

153. Schmitt Davidson, Houghton University athletic event.

154. Daniel R. Chamberlain, sermon at Houghton College campus memorial service, October 7, 1981, audio recording and manuscript. Houghton University Archives.

155. Shire Hildebrandt, interview.

156. Katie Singer and Deb Price, *Houghton Star*, October 9, 1981.

157. Cindy Brenner Dey, text messages to author, February 4, 2024.

158. The story of the volleyball team's collision with the cow was shared by Cindy Brenner Dey (text messages to author, February 4, 2024), Katie Singer and Deb Price (*Houghton Star*, October 9, 1981) and Charles Massey (Solovitch, "Homecoming Plans").

159. Shire Hildebrandt, interview.

160. Singer and Price, *Houghton Star*.

161. Judy Tennant Mahoney, interview with author, October 9, 2023.

162. Barbara Bushart, interview.

163. Meg Martino Wright, email messages with author, January 2024.

164. Fuller Bowling, interview.

165. Gifford, interview.

166. Houghton College, "Personal data form" for Cindy Rudes, September 1981, Houghton University Archives.

167. Schmitt Davidson, Houghton University athletic event.

168. Cindy Rudes, "Good-bye at Halim," *The Alliance Witness*, December 9, 1981, 26.

169. Jim Redmond and David Galante, "6 Houghton Students Killed," *Rochester Democrat & Chronicle*, October 3, 1981.

OCTOBER 2, 1981

1. *Houghton College Catalog*, 1981, 17.
2. Allen Hemayakian, interview with author, October 17, 2023.
3. Jan Merz Kennedy, interview with author, October 6, 2023.
4. Ed Taylor, interview with author, October 12, 2023.
5. Brian Segool, email message to author, October 2023.
6. Warren Bushart, interview with author, November 13, 2016.
7. *breakfast in the campus center*: Judy Tennant Mahoney, interview with author, October 9, 2023.
8. Ruth Hutton, "The Ultimate Homecoming," *Moody Monthly*, March 1982, 134.
9. Katie Singer and Deb Price, *Houghton Star*, October 9, 1981.
10. Marlene Gifford, interview with author, October 24, 2023.
11. Susan Facer, personal correspondence to Mr. and Mrs. Bert Anderson, October 18, 1982.
12. Mercy Zecher Dawson, email messages to author, January–February, 2024.
13. Karyn Hecht, email messages to author, January–February, 2024.
14. Hemayakian, interview.
15. *Bert had invited*: Taylor, interview.
16. Meg Martino Wright, email messages to author, January 2024.
17. Gifford, interview.
18. Mr. Bingenheimer's name and these other basic facts about him were included in multiple news reports.
19. Information about the students' seating arrangement and clothing is taken from the Erie County Sheriff's accident report.
20. Keith Epstein, "The Ripples Cast by an 'Ordinary' Life," *Watertown Daily Times*, October 13, 1981.
21. "A Joy Forever," 2021, 7. Houghton University Archives.
22. Marshall J. Brown, "6 Students Killed in Auto Collision," *Buffalo Courier Express*, October 3, 1981.
23. Michael Levy, "6 Deaths May Spur Road Signal," *Buffalo Evening News*, October 7, 1981.
24. Ron Becker, interview with author, December 14, 2023.
25. Hutton, "Ultimate Homecoming," 134–135.
26. Although slightly different times were reported in the press, this is the time noted in the accident report.
27. Sara Solovitch, "Homecoming Plans Led to Fatal Journey," *Buffalo Courier Express*, October 3, 1981.
28. *Olean Times Herald*, "Six Houghton College Students Killed in 'Worst-Ever' Accident," October 3, 1981.
29. Brown, "6 Students Killed."
30. *Sunday Spectator*, "Fatal Crash Stuns Houghton Campus," October 4, 1981.
31. Brown, "6 Students Killed."
32. Erie County Sheriff's accident report, October 2, 1981.
33. Brown, "6 Students Killed."
34. Solovitch, "Homecoming Plans."

35. Brown, "6 Students Killed."
36. Ron Becker, interview with author, December 14, 2023.
37. Larry Mullen, interview with author, November 1, 2023.
38. Gene Warner, "Houghton Grieves During Rites for Six Crash Victims," *Buffalo News*, October 3, 1981.
39. Brown, "6 Students Killed."
40. Becker, interview.
41. *Olean Times Herald*, "Six Houghton College Students."
42. Brown, "6 Students Killed."
43. Erie County Sheriff's accident report.
44. Modesto Argenio, "A Sheriff Who Can Still Cry," *Buffalo Evening News*, October 8, 1981.
45. *"You mean all six are gone!"*: Ruth Hutton, "The Ultimate Homecoming, *Moody Monthly*, March 1982, 135. The remainder of the meeting description is from the author's interview with Robert Danner, September 1, 2016.
46. Danner, interview.
47. Mark Abbott, email message to author, September 2016.
48. Danner, interview.
49. Sandy Roederer, interview with author, October 14, 2023.
50. Fred Shannon, interview with author, October 13, 2023.
51. Danner, interview.
52. Daniel Chamberlain and Evelyn Bence, "The Homecoming," *Christian Herald*, October 1982, 26.
53. Chamberlain and Bence, "Homecoming," 26.
54. Tim Nichols, interview with author, October 12, 2023.
55. Warren and Barbara Bushart, interview with author, November 13, 2016.
56. Warren and Barbara Bushart, interview.
57. Kevin Bushart, email message to author, December 2016.
58. Solovitch, "Homecoming Plans."
59. Debbie Rudes Haas, interview with author, November 28, 2023.
60. Bud and Ruth Rudes, "The Month of October, 1981," November 1981.
61. Rudes Haas, interview.
62. Mindy Andes, interview with author, January 21, 2024.
63. Solovitch, "Homecoming Plans."
64. Chamberlain and Bence, "Homecoming," 28.
65. Daniel R. Chamberlain, interview with author, January 16, 2024.
66. Chamberlain, interview.
67. Keith Anderson, interview with author, October 5, 2023.
68. Terry Anderson, interview with author, October 3, 2023.
69. Charles Massey, interview with author, October 31, 2023.
70. Danner, interview.
71. Carol Stevens, "Houghton Deals with Deaths," *Buffalo Courier Express*, October 4, 1981.
72. Nichols, interview.
73. Many students remember hearing the WJSL announcement. The specific time comes from the reporting of Carol Stevens in the *Buffalo Courier Express*, "Houghton Deals with Deaths," October 4, 1981.

74. Jim Redmond and David Galante, "6 Houghton Students Killed," *Rochester Democrat & Chronicle*, October 3, 1981.
75. Kathie Brenneman, interview with author, October 2016.
76. Nichols, interview.
77. Meg Martino Wright, email messages to author, January 2024.
78. Doug Burke, interview with author, February 9, 2024.
79. Hutton, "Ultimate Homecoming," 135.
80. Cindy Brenner Dey, text messages to author, February 4, 2024.
81. Merz Kennedy, interview.
82. Mary Beth Fuller Bowling, interview with author, November 13, 2023.
83. Hecht, email.
84. Richard "Jake" Jacobsen, interview with author, February 8, 2017.
85. Connie Finney, interview with author, October 30, 2023.
86. Becca Thorn Oehrig, email message to author, November 2016.
87. Hemayakian, interview.
88. Gifford, interview.
89. Zecher Dawson, email.
90. Segool, email.
91. Erma Mekeel Boswell, email message to author, November 2016.
92. Mark Ohl, email message to author, October 2023.
93. Hutton, "Ultimate Homecoming," 134.
94. Taylor, interview.
95. Solovitch, "Homecoming Plans."
96. This account comes from Larry Mullen (interview with author, November 1, 2023) and Harold Kingdon (email message to author, October 5, 2023).
97. Graham Drake, interview with author, November 8, 2023.
98. Bread, "Everything I Own," track 4 on *Baby I'm-a Want You,* Elektra, 1972.
99. Warner, "Houghton Grieves."
100. Dexter Davis, interview with author, September 26, 2023.
101. Abbott, email.
102. Stevens, "Houghton Deals."
103. Abbott, email.
104. Danner, interview.
105. Unless otherwise noted, all quotations and accounts of the Friday evening campus gathering in Wesley Chapel come from the audio recording of the service located in the Houghton University Archives.
106. Horatio Spafford, "It Is Well with My Soul," 1873.
107. John Fawcett, "Blest Be the Tie That Binds," 1782.
108. Andrae Crouch, "Through It All," 1971.
109. Thorn Oehrig, email.
110. Gifford, interview.
111. Redmond and Galante, "6 Houghton Students."
112. Brenneman, interview.
113. Jim Redmond, "Deaths Unite Campus," *Rochester Democrat & Chronicle,* October 4, 1981.
114. Warner, "Houghton Grieves."
115. Stevens, "Houghton Deals."

116. Fuller Bowling, interview.
117. Author's personal recollection.
118. Gifford, interview.
119. Ohl, email.
120. Chamberlain and Bence, "Homecoming," 28.
121. Kevin Bushart, email.

AFTERMATH

1. Daniel R. Chamberlain, personal correspondence to his family, October 12, 1981.
2. Mercy Zecher Dawson, email messages to author, January–February 2024.
3. Richard "Jake" Jacobsen, interview with author, February 8, 2017.
4. Marlene Gifford, interview with author, October 24, 2023.
5. Ed Taylor, interview with author, October 12, 2023.
6. "Services Slated for Houghton Students," *Olean Times Herald,* October 5, 1981.
7. Mark Ohl, email message to author, October 2023.
8. Tedd Smith, interview with author, October 6, 2023.
9. Brian Segool, email message to author, October 2023.
10. Rob Ruth, interview with author, November 8, 2023.
11. Segool, email.
12. Mark Abbott, email message to author, September 2016.
13. Ruth Hutton, "The Ultimate Homecoming," *Moody Monthly*, March 1982, 135.
14. Hutton, "Ultimate Homecoming," 136.
15. Daniel R. Chamberlain, interview conducted by Dean Liddick, August 11, 2011.
16. "Accident Claims 6 Houghton Students," *Tonawanda News,* October 3, 1981.
17. Carol Stevens, "Houghton Deals with Deaths," *Buffalo Courier Express*, October 4, 1981.
18. "Services Slated," *Olean Times Herald.*
19. *Attendance in classes was light*: Hutton, "Ultimate Homecoming," 136.
20. "Houghton to Proceed with Homecoming," *Buffalo Evening News,* October 7, 1981.
21. Stevens, "Houghton Deals."
22. Gifford, interview.
23. David Frazier, interview with author, October 3, 2023.
24. "Houghton to Proceed," *Buffalo Evening News.*
25. Robert Danner, interview with author, September 1, 2016.
26. Dean Liddick, interview with author, October 12, 2023.
27. Jim Redmond, "Deaths Unite Campus," *Rochester Democrat & Chronicle,* October 4, 1981.
28. Redmond, "Deaths Unite Campus."
29. Joan Dickensen, "Houghton Students Extol Spirit of 6 Crash Victims," *Buffalo Courier Express,* October 11, 1981.
30. Hutton, "Ultimate Homecoming," 136.
31. Hutton, "Ultimate Homecoming," 135.
32. Keith Anderson, interview with author, October 5, 2023.
33. Terry Anderson, interview with author, October 3, 2023.
34. Hutton, "Ultimate Homecoming," 137.

35. Mary Beth Fuller Bowling, interview with author, November 13, 2023; Marlene Gifford, interview with author, October 24, 2023.
36. Mindy Andes, interview with author, January 21, 2024.
37. Zecher Dawson, email.
38. Warren and Barbara Bushart, interview with author, November 13, 2016.
39. *shattered*: Tim Nichols, interview with author, October 12, 2023; *as the closing song started*: Barbara Bushart, interview with author, November 13, 2016.
40. Kevin Bushart, email message to author, December 2016.
41. Debbie Rudes Haas, interview with author, November 28, 2023.
42. Gifford, interview.
43. Bud and Ruth Rudes, "The Month of October, 1981," November 1981.
44. Betty Bowser Young, interview with author, November 22, 2023.
45. Frazier, interview.
46. C. S. Lewis, *The Last Battle,* (New York: HarperCollins, 2000), 210.
47. Taylor, interview.
48. Jan Merz Kennedy, interview with author, October 6, 2023.
49. Keith C. Epstein, "Six 'Live' in Friends' Hearts." *Watertown Daily Times,* October 8, 1981.
50. Messages of condolence, Houghton University Archives.
51. Hutton, "Ultimate Homecoming," 136.
52. Danner, interview.
53. Charles Massey, interview with author, October 31, 2023.
54. Ray Hill, "Houghton Binds Its Wounds," *Buffalo News,* October 11, 1981.
55. Massey, interview.
56. Daniel Chamberlain, audio recording of campus memorial service, October 7, 1981, Houghton University Archives.
57. Massey, interview.
58. Bert Freed, "Memory of 6 Students Killed in Car Crash Mourned at Houghton," *Buffalo Evening News,* October 8, 1981.
59. Sue Goetschius, "A Service of Worship and Hope," *Olean Times Herald,* October 8, 1981.
60. Liddick, interview.
61. Campus memorial service printed program, October 7, 1981, Houghton University Archives.
62. *"clutching handkerchiefs"*: Epstein, "Six 'Live.'"
63. Unless otherwise noted, all quotations and accounts of the campus memorial service come from the audio recording of the service located in the Houghton University Archives.
64. Caroline V. Sandell-Berg, "Children of the Heavenly Father," 1849.
65. James Leith MacBeth Bain, "Brother James' Air," 1915.
66. Isaac Watts, "O God Our Help in Ages Past," 1708.
67. Jon Horton, email message to author, October 2023.
68. Samuel Trevor Francis, "O the Deep, Deep Love of Jesus," 1875.
69. Goetschius, "Worship and Hope."
70. Segool, email.
71. Bud and Ruth Rudes, "Month of October, 1981."
72. Doug Roorbach, email message to author, November 2023.

73. Goetschius, "Worship and Hope."
74. Rudes Haas, interview.
75. Hutton, "Ultimate Homecoming," 137.
76. Goetschius, "Worship and Hope."
77. *Houghton Star*, October 9, 1981.
78. Goetschius, "Worship and Hope."
79. Goetschius, "Worship and Hope."
80. "Officials to Discuss Hazardous Intersection in Wales," *Buffalo Courier Express*, October 4, 1981.
81. Michel Levy, "6 Deaths May Spur Road Signal," *Buffalo Evening News*, October 7, 1981.
82. Levy, "6 Deaths."
83. Robert Kowalewski, "Call for Action," *East Aurora Advertiser*, October 15, 1981.
84. Lew Smith, "Businessmen Call for Signals," *East Aurora Advertiser*, October 15, 1981.
85. Norman Erint, letter to Erie County Sheriff's Office, October 5, 1981. Included in accident report.
86. "Too Late," *East Aurora Advertiser*, October 8, 1981.
87. Hill, "Houghton Binds."
88. Epstein, "Six 'Live.'"
89. "Services Slated," *Olean Times Herald.*
90. Daniel R. Chamberlain, audio recording of Founder's Day chapel, October 9, 1981, Houghton University Archives.
91. *Houghton Star*, October 9, 1981.
92. *Houghton Star*, October 9, 1981.
93. *Houghton Star*, October 9, 1981.
94. "Tragedy Mars but Won't Halt Houghton's Weekend," *Olean Times Herald*, October 8, 1981.
95. Hill, "Houghton Binds."
96. Houghton College, *Boulder*, 1982, 117–121.
97. Dickenson, "Houghton Students Extol."
98. Judy Tennant Mahoney, interview with author, October 9, 2023.
99. Gifford, interview.
100. Stevens, "Houghton Deals."
101. Dexter Davis, interview with author, September 26, 2023.
102. Hill, "Houghton Binds."
103. Hill, "Houghton Binds."
104. The reading of this poem at the Senate Spot was noted in Hill, "Houghton Binds." The text of the poem is taken from the 1982 Houghton College *Boulder*, 117–121.
105. Ohl, email.
106. Merz Kennedy, interview.
107. Becca Thorn Oehrig, email message to author, November 2016.
108. Hill, "Houghton Binds."
109. Hutton, "Ultimate Homecoming," 136.
110. "Six Seniors at Houghton College Killed When Their Car, Truck Collide," *Christian College News*, October 9, 1981, 2.

111. Hill, "Houghton Binds."
112. Graham Drake, interview with author, November 8, 2023.

EMPTY SEATS AND FRIDAY FLOWERS

1. Keith C. Epstein, "The Ripples Cast by an 'Ordinary' Life," *Watertown Daily Times*, October 13, 1981.
2. C. S. Lewis, *A Grief Observed,* (New York: The Seabury Press, 1961), 7.
3. Andrew Mullen, email messages to author, January 2024.
4. Betty Bowser Young, interview with author, November 22, 2023.
5. Richard "Jake" Jacobsen, interview with author, February 8, 2017.
6. Brian Segool, email message to author, October 2023.
7. Graham Drake, interview with author, November 8, 2023.
8. Mullen, email.
9. "Jake" Jacobsen, interview.
10. Warren and Barbara Bushart, interview with author, November 13, 2016.
11. Ray Parlett, interview with author, October 12, 2023.
12. Bowser Young, interview.
13. Mary Beth Fuller Bowling, interview with author, November 13, 2023.
14. Jan Merz Kennedy, interview with author, October 6, 2023.
15. Marlene Gifford, interview with author, October 24, 2023.
16. Parlett, interview.
17. Ruth Hutton, "The Ultimate Homecoming," *Moody Monthly,* March 1982, 135.
18. David Frazier, interview with author, October 3, 2023.
19. Bill Doezema, focus group discussion with author, November 13, 2023.
20. Daniel R. Chamberlain, personal correspondence to his family, October 12, 1981.
21. Daniel R. Chamberlain, personal correspondence to Mr. and Mrs. Bert Anderson, October 15, 1981.
22. Debbie Rudes Haas, interview with author, November 28, 2023.
23. Bud and Ruth Rudes, "The Month of October, 1981," November 1981.
24. Rudes Haas, interview.
25. Terry Anderson, interview with author, October 5, 2023.
26. Keith Anderson, interview with author, October 3, 2023.
27. Mindy Andes, interview with author, January 21, 2024.
28. Warren and Barbara Bushart, interview.
29. Rob Jacobsen, interview with author, November 13, 2023.
30. Mercy Zecher Dawson, email messages with author, January–February, 2024.
31. Andrew Mullen, email.
32. Gifford, interview.
33. Mullen, email.
34. Betsy Lundell Carosa, interview with author, January 4, 2024.
35. Allen Hemayakian, interview with author, October 17, 2023.
36. Tim Nichols, interview with author, October 12, 2023.
37. Jim Redmond, "Deaths Unite Campus," *Rochester Democrat & Chronicle,* October 4, 1981.
38. Mullen, email.

39. Meg Martino Wright, email messages with author, January 2024.

40. Glenn Burlingame, interview with author, December 3, 2023.

41. Daniel R. Chamberlain, interview conducted by Dean Liddick, August 11, 2011.

42. Houghton College, *Boulder,* 1982, 210.

43. Houghton College, *Boulder*, 1982, 228.

44. Dean Liddick, "Myline," *Houghton Milieu*, November 1981, 2.

45. Arnold Kenseth, "Canticles Autumn" in *Sabbath, Sacraments and Seasons*, (Philadelphia: Pilgrim Press, 1969), 160.

46. "Student Killed," *Houghton Milieu,* January 1982, 11. Mark Schiefer was also memorialized with a tribute on page 113 of the 1982 *Boulder*.

47. Steve Dunbar, email message to author, November 2016.

48. Daniel R. Chamberlain, interview with author, January 16, 2024.

49. Rob Jacobsen, interview.

50. Tom Kettlekamp, focus group discussion with author, November 13, 2023.

51. Karyn Hecht, email message to author, March 22, 2024.

52. "A Joy Forever," 2021, 20. Houghton University Archives.

53. Remarks made at commencement come from the audio tape of the commencement exercises located in the Houghton University Archives.

54. *ten members*: Bert Freed, "6 Posthumous Degrees Given at Houghton College Graduation," *Buffalo Evening News*, October 12, 1981.

55. Redmond, "Deaths Unite Campus."

56. The memorial section of the 1982 *Boulder* is found on pages 18–23.

MAKING SENSE OF SUFFERING

1. William Shakespeare, *MacBeth*, Alfred Harbage, ed. (New York: Viking Press, 1969), 5.5.24–28. Andrew Mullen pointed out to me the connection between the accident and these words from Shakespeare.

2. "Like a River Glorious," Frances Ridley Havergal, 1874.

3. Daniel R. Chamberlain, notes from remarks given at eagles sculpture dedication, October 11, 1986. Houghton University Archives.

4. Daniel R. Chamberlain, interview with author, January 16, 2024.

5. Dean Liddick, "They Shall Mount Up with Wings as Eagles," *Houghton Milieu*, September 1986, 28.

6. "A Remembrance," *Gloucester County Times*, September 9, 1986.

7. Daniel R. Chamberlain, eagles sculpture remarks.

8. Andrew Mullen, email messages to author, January 2024.

9. Judy Tennant Mahoney, interview with author, October 9, 2023.

10. Marlene Gifford, interview with author, October 24, 2023.

11. Charles Massey, interview with author, October 31, 2023.

12. Robert Danner, interview with author, September 1, 2016.

13. Bud Bence, email message to author, February 28, 2024.

14. All quotations from and descriptions of the twenty-fifth anniversary service come from the audio recording of the service located in the Houghton University Archives.

15. Post-service activities are described in *Cuba Patriot and Free Press*, "Houghton Community Remembers Homecoming 1981," October 11–17, 2016.

16. Tim Nichols, "Forever 20, a Generation Later," *Houghton Milieu*, Fall 2006, 2.

17. Daniel Noyes, "The Start of a New Tradition," *Houghton Magazine*, Spring/Summer 2010, 23.

18. Many years ago I heard a sermon by John Ortberg at Willow Creek Community Church that inspired this line of thinking; I do not recall the date or title of the sermon.

19. Shirley Mullen, email message to author, April 5, 2024.

20. These quotes are typical of those made by so many people that I am not listing specific names here.

21. Terry Anderson, interview with author, October 3, 2023.

22. Debbie Rudes Haas, interview with author, November 28, 2023.

23. Kevin Danielson, social media message to author, April 18, 2024.

24. Rudes Haas, interview.

25. Glenn Burlingame, interview with author, December 3, 2023.

26. Burlingame, interview.

27. Mindy Andes, interview with author, January 21, 2024.

28. Ray Parlett, interview with author, October 12, 2023.

29. Terry Anderson, interview.

30. Nicholas Wolterstorff, *Lament for a Son* (Grand Rapids, MI: William B. Eerdmans Publishing, Co.), 68.

31. Rudes Haas, interview.

32. Tim Nichols, interview with author, October 12, 2023.

33. Betty Bowser Young, interview with author, November 22, 2023.

34. Gifford, interview.

35. Mary Beth Fuller Bowling, interview with author, November 13, 2023.

36. Gifford, interview.

37. Parlett, interview.

38. Betsy Lundell Carosa, interview with author, January 4, 2024.

39. Steve Dunbar, email message to author, November 2016.

40. Burlingame, interview.

41. Kevin Bushart, email message to author, December 2016.

42. Rudes Haas, interview.

43. Andrew Mullen, email.

44. Nichols, interview.

45. Jeff Jordan, email message to author, September 21, 2023.

46. Tennant Mahoney, interview.

47. Brian Segool, email message to author, October 2023.

48. Rudes Haas, interview.

49. Annie Dillard, *The Abundance* (New York: HarperCollins, 2016), 189.

50. Jan Merz Kennedy, interview with author, October 6, 2023.

51. Tennant Mahoney, interview.

52. Rob Jacobsen, interview with author, November 13, 2023.

53. Andes, interview.

54. Kevin Bushart, email.

55. Barbara Bushart, interview with author, November 13, 2016.

56. Rudes Haas, interview.

57. Daniel Chamberlain and Evelyn Bence, "The Homecoming," *Christian Herald,* October 1982, 30.

58. Chamberlain, interview with author.

59. Kirsten Dyal Barton, email message to author, November 9, 2023.

60. Gifford, interview.

61. Becca Thorn Oehrig, email message to author, November 2016.

62. Burlingame, interview.

63. Nichols, "Forever 20."

64. Fuller Bowling, interview.

65. Burlingame, interview.

66. Merz Kennedy, interview.

67. Nichols, interview.

68. Steve Jacobsen, email message to author, March 1, 2024.

69. Merz Kennedy, interview.

70. Bert and Doris Anderson, personal correspondence, 2006.

71. Merz Kennedy, interview.

72. Dyal Barton, email.

73. Mark Abbott, email message to author, September 2016.

74. Andes, interview.

75. Graham Drake, interview with author, November 8, 2023.

76. Dunbar, email.

77. Bill Allen, email message to author, November 2016.

78. Connie Finney, interview with author, October 30, 2023.

79. Gifford, interview.

80. Martha Manikas-Foster, email message to author, November 2023.

81. This unique sadness was shared with me by a sibling of one of The Six, but that person's name is not being shared as a courtesy to the family.

82. Bert and Doris Anderson, correspondence.

83. *"Until we reach eternity"*: Dexter Davis, interview with author, September 26, 2023; *"I often think about"*: Marlene Gifford, interview with author, October 24, 2023; *"Only eternity"*: Steve Dunbar, email message to author, November 2016.

84. Tedd Smith, interview with author, October 6, 2023.

85. Brian and Chris Davidson, remarks at Houghton University athletic event attended by author, October 21, 2023.

86. Barbara Bushart, interview with author, November 13, 2016.

87. Jeff Jordan, email message to author, September 21, 2023.

88. Merz Kennedy, interview.

89. Rudes Haas, interview.

90. Kevin Bushart, email.

91. This phrase is the title of one of Henri Nouwen's most beloved books.

92. Information about endowed funds was provided by the Houghton University Office of Advancement and with donor permission.

93. Martha Manikas-Foster, email message to author, November 2023.

94. Manikas-Foster, email.

95. On one of my visits to the intersection in the fall of 2023, a middle-aged gentleman was in the yard of a house near the intersection and inquired about

why I was walking around the area. When I told him about my research for this book, he made this comment. He lived in the house as a small boy at the time of the accident, and the house remains with his family to this day.

POSTSCRIPT: TEARS IN A BOTTLE

1. This quotation from Thomas Merton is transcribed from the audio recording of the twenty-fifth anniversary service. Unfortunately, I have been unable to locate the original quote in Merton's writings and regret that I cannot give precise attribution in Merton's work.
2. Barbara Brown Taylor, *Learning to Walk in the Dark,* (New York: HarperCollins, 2014), 7.
3. Brown Taylor, *Learning to Walk,* 9.
4. Dorothy Sayers, "The Greatest Drama Ever Staged" in *Christian Letters to a Post-Christian World,* Roderick Jellema, ed. (Grand Rapids: William B. Eerdmans Publishing Co., 1969), 14.
5. Nicholas Wolterstorff, *Lament for a Son* (Grand Rapids: William B. Eerdmans Publishing Co., 1987), 81.

BIBLIOGRAPHY

As a convenience to the readers, I am dividing this bibliography into three sections. In the first section, I list all books and periodicals that were utilized in the research for this book. The second section includes all archival materials, correspondence, journal entries, recordings and musical selections to which I refer. The final section provides a list of the people with whom I have spoken about these events, either in person, by phone, or via email/texting.

BOOKS AND PERIODICALS

Anderson, Mark. "Maintaining Open Forum." *Houghton Star.* September 18, 1981.

Argenio, Modesto. "A Sheriff Who Can Still Cry." *Buffalo Evening News.* October 8, 1981.

Brown, Marshall J. "6 Students Killed in Auto Collision." *Buffalo Courier Express.* October 3, 1981.

Brown, Mickey. "Solemnity Marks 82nd Houghton Commencement." *Olean Times Herald.* May 11, 1982.

Buffalo Courier Express. "Officials to Discuss Hazardous Intersection in Wales." October 4, 1981.

Buffalo Evening News. "Houghton to Proceed with Homecoming." October 7, 1981.

Burlingame, Glenn and Linda Ippolito (eds.). *Houghton Star.* October 9, 1981.

Chamberlain, Daniel R. and Evelyn Bence. "The Homecoming." *Christian Herald.* October 1982.

Chamberlain, Mark E. *Daniel and Joyce Chamberlain: Faithful to God and Family*. Self-published. 2022.

Christian College News. "Six Seniors at Houghton College Killed When Their Car, Truck Collide." October 9, 1981.

Clark, Debbie. "Houghton: Tragedy, Sorrow." *Olean Times Herald*. October 3, 1981.

Cuba Patriot and Free Press. "Houghton Community Remembers Homecoming 1981." October 11–17, 2016.

Davis, Marsha. "Those Who Knew Her Recall Victim as 'Joy.'" *Watertown Daily Times*. October 3, 1981.

Dickenson, Joan. "Houghton Students Extol Spirit of 6 Crash Victims." *Buffalo Courier Express*. October 11, 1981.

Dillard, Annie. *The Abundance*. New York: Harper Collins, 2016.

East Aurora Advertiser. "20A Fatality Incites Outcry of Officials." October 8, 1981.

East Aurora Advertiser. "Too Late" letter to the editor. October 8, 1981.

Epstein, Keith C. "Six 'Live' in Friends' Hearts." *Watertown Daily Times*. October 8, 1981.

Epstein, Keith C. "The Ripples Cast by an 'Ordinary' Life." *Watertown Daily Times*. October 13, 1981.

Finger Lakes Times (Geneva, NY). "Former Genevan Among 6 Killed." October 3, 1981.

Freed, Bert. "Memory of 6 Students Killed in Car Crash Mourned at Houghton." *Buffalo Evening News*. October 8, 1981.

Freed, Bert. "Homecoming Opening Subdued at Houghton." *Buffalo Evening News*. October 12, 1981.

Freed, Bert. "6 Posthumous Degrees Given at Houghton College Graduation." *Buffalo Evening News*. May 11, 1982.

Gloucester County Times. "A Remembrance," September 9, 1986.

Goetschius, Sue. "A Service of Worship and Hope." *Olean Times Herald*. October 8, 1981.

Hill, Ray. "Houghton Binds Its Wounds." *Buffalo News*. October 11, 1981.

Houghton Milieu. "Tragedy, Triumph and the Ultimate Homecoming." November 1981.

Houghton Milieu. "Student Killed." January 1982.

Hutton, Ruth. "The Ultimate Homecoming." *Moody Monthly.* March 1982.

Journal-Register (Medina, NY). "Memorial Service Set for Six Students Killed in Crash." October 5, 1981.

Kenseth, Arnold. *Sabbaths, Sacraments and Seasons.* Philadelphia: Pilgrim Press, 1969.

Kowalewski, Robert L. "Call for Action," *East Aurora Advertiser.* October 15, 1981.

Levy, Michael. "6 Deaths May Spur Road Signal." *Buffalo Evening News.* October 7, 1981.

Lewis, C. S. *A Grief Observed.* New York: The Seabury Press, 1961.

Lewis, C. S. *The Last Battle.* New York: HarperCollins, 2000.

Liddick, Dean. "Myline." *Houghton Milieu.* November 1981.

Liddick, Dean. "They Shall Mount Up with Wings as Eagles." *Houghton Milieu.* September 1986.

Nichols, Tim. "Forever 20, a Generation Later." *Houghton Milieu.* Fall 2006.

Noyes, Daniel. "The Start of a New Tradition." *Houghton Magazine.* Spring/ Summer 2020.

Olean Times Herald. "Six Houghton College Students Killed in 'Worst-Ever' Accident." October 3, 1981.

Olean Times Herald. "Services Slated for Houghton Students." October 5, 1981.

Olean Times Herald. "Tragedy Mars but Won't Halt Houghton's Weekend." October 8, 1981.

New York Times. "6 College Students Killed in Collision." October 3, 1981.

Palladium-Times (Oswego, NY). "Six College Students Killed in Crash." October 3, 1981.

Redmond, Jim. "Deaths Unite Campus." *Rochester Democrat & Chronicle.* October 4, 1981.

Redmond, Jim and David Galante. "6 Houghton Students Killed." *Rochester Democrat & Chronicle.* October 3, 1981.

Rochester Democrat & Chronicle. "Words of Comfort." October 4, 1981.

Rudes, Cindy. "Good-bye at Halim." *The Alliance Witness.* December 9, 1981. Published posthumously.

Sayers, Dorothy. "The Greatest Drama Ever Staged" in *Christian Letters to a*

Post-Christian World. Roderick Jellema, ed. Grand Rapids, MI: William B. Eerdmans Publishing Co., 1969.

Shakespeare, William. *MacBeth.* Alfred Harbage, ed. New York: Viking Press, 1969.

Smith, Lew. "Businessmen Call for Signals." *East Aurora Advertiser.* October 15, 1981.

Solovitch, Sara. "Homecoming Plans Led to Fatal Journey." *Buffalo Courier Express.* October 3, 1981.

Stevens, Carol. "Houghton Deals with Deaths." *Buffalo Courier Express.* October 4, 1981.

Sunday Spectator (Hornell, NY). "Fatal Crash Stuns Houghton Campus." October 4, 1981.

Taylor, Barbara Brown. *Learning to Walk in the Dark.* New York: HarperCollins, 2014.

Tonawanda News. "Accident Claims 6 Houghton Students." October 3, 1981.

Vogel, Mike and Dennis Hollins. "Six Killed in Truck-Car Collision." *Buffalo Evening News.*October 2, 1981.

Warner, Gene. "Houghton Grieves During Rites for Six Crash Victims." *Buffalo News.* October 3, 1981.

Watertown Daily Times. "City Pastor's Daughter Killed in 'Worst' Crash." October 3, 1981.

Wolterstorff, Nicholas. *Lament for a Son.* Grand Rapids, MI: William B. Eerdmans Publishing Co., 1987.

ARCHIVAL MATERIAL, PERSONAL DOCUMENTS, AND MUSICAL SELECTIONS

Anderson, Bert and Doris. Personal correspondence. 2006. Provided by Anderson family.

Anderson, Mark. Personal journal. 1981. Provided by Anderson family.

Anderson, Mark. Notes from undated speech given at Houghton College. Provided by Anderson family.

Bain, James Leith MacBeth. "Brother James' Air." 1915.

Boulder. Houghton College. 1982.

Bread. "Everything I Own." Track 4 on *Baby I'm-a Want You*. Elektra. 1972.

Chamberlain, Daniel R. Personal correspondence to family. October 12, 1981. Provided by Chamberlain family.

Chamberlain, Daniel R. Personal correspondence to Bert and Doris Anderson. October 15, 1981. Provided by Anderson family.

Crouch, Andrae. "Through It All." 1971.

Erie County Sheriff's Accident Report. October 2, 1981. Received February 5, 2024.

Facer, Susan. Personal correspondence to Mr. and Mrs. Bert Anderson, October 18, 1982. Provided by Anderson family.

Fawcett, John. "Blest Be the Tie That Binds." 1782.

Francis, Samuel Trevor. "O the Deep, Deep Love of Jesus." 1875.

Havergal, Frances Ridley. "Like a River Glorious." 1874.

Hawkins, Rich. Personal correspondence to Mr. and Mrs. Bert Anderson. May 6, 1982. Provided by Anderson family.

Houghton College Catalog. 1981.

Houghton University Archives. "A Joy Forever." Anonymous essay. October 2021.

———. Audio recording of campus meeting. October 2, 1981.

———. Audio recording of campus memorial service. October 7, 1981.

———. Audio recording of Founder's Day Chapel. October 9, 1981.

———. Audio recording of Commencement. May 10, 1982.

———. Audio recording of twenty-fifth anniversary service. October 2, 2006.

———. Cards, letters, and telegrams sent to Houghton College. October 1981.

———. Letter from Barry Conboy of Hudson City Savings Bank. October 5, 1981.

———. Photographs from 1981–82 academic year.

———. Press release: "Houghton College Announces Homecoming Events." October 5, 1981.

———. Press release: "Houghton Accident Victims Memorialized." October 8, 1981.

———. Press release: "Memorialized Students' Biographies." October 8, 1981

———. Printed program of campus memorial service. October 7, 1981.

———. Student data forms for Mark Anderson, Beth Andes, Alan Bushart, Joy

Ellis, Bert Rapp, Cindy Rudes. September 1981.

———. Video recording of Dr. Daniel Chamberlain interview (Dean Liddick, interviewer). August 11, 2011.

———. Dr. Daniel Chamberlain notes from remarks given at eagles sculpture dedication. October 11, 1986.

Houghton University Athletics Department. Video recording of event honoring Alan Bushart, Joy Ellis, and Cindy Rudes. October 21, 2023.

Rudes, Bud and Ruth. "The Month of October, 1981." Correspondence to friends and supporters. November 1981. Provided by Debbie Rudes Haas.

Sandell-Berg, Caroline V. "Children of the Heavenly Father." 1849.

Spafford, Horatio. "It Is Well with My Soul." 1873.

Watts, Isaac. "O God Our Help in Ages Past." 1708.

PERSONAL CONVERSATIONS

Abbott, Mark. Email message to author. September 2016.

Allen, Bill. Email message to author. November 2016.

Anderson, Keith. Interview conducted by author. October 5, 2023.

Anderson, Terry. Interview conducted by author. October 3, 2023.

Andes, Mindy. Interview conducted by author. January 21, 2024.

Austin, Cindy Prentice. Email message to author. November 2023.

Barton, Kirsten Dyal. Email message to author. November 9, 2023.

Becker, Ron. Interview conducted by author. December 14, 2023.

Bence, Bud. Email message to author. February 28, 2024.

Boswell, Erma Mekeel. Email message to author. November 2016.

Bowling, Mary Beth Fuller. Interview conducted by author. November 13, 2023.

Bradley, Jon. Social media message to author. October 21, 2023.

Brenneman, Kathie. Interview conducted by author. October 2016.

Burke, Doug. Interview conducted by author. February 9, 2024.

Burlingame, Glenn. Interview conducted by author. December 3, 2023.

Bushart, Barbara Isaman. Interview conducted by author. November 13, 2016.

Bushart, Kevin. Email message to author. December 2016.

Bushart, Warren. Interview conducted by author. November 13, 2016.

Carosa, Betsy Lundell. Interview conducted by author. January 4, 2024.

Chamberlain, Daniel R. Interview conducted by author. January 16, 2024.

Christopher, Mark. Text messages to author. September 2023.

Danielson, Kevin. Social media message to author. April 28, 2024.

Danner, Robert. Interview conducted by author. September 1, 2016.

Davidson, Brian. Athletics event attended by author. October 21, 2023.

Davidson, Chris Schmitt. Athletics event attended by author. October 21, 2023.

Davis, Dexter. Interview conducted by author. September 26, 2023

Dawson, Mercy Zecher. Email messages to author. January–February 2024.

Dey, Cindy Brenner. Text messages to author. February 4, 2024.

Doezema, Bill. Participant in focus group discussion with author. November 13, 2023.

Drake, Graham. Interview conducted by author. November 8, 2023.

Dunbar, Steve. Email message to author. November 2016.

Finney, Connie. Interview conducted by author. October 30, 2023.

Frazier, David. Interview conducted by author. October 3, 2023.

Gifford, Marlene. Interview conducted by author. October 24, 2023.

Haas, Debbie Rudes. Interview conducted by author. November 28, 2023.

Hansen, Kristina. Email message to author. November 2023.

Hecht, Karyn. Email messages to author. January–February 2024.

Hemayakian, Allen. Interview conducted by author. October 17, 2023.

Hildebrandt, Tanya Shire. Interview conducted by author. October 27, 2023.

Horton, Jon. Email message to author. October 2023.

Jacobsen, Richard "Jake." Interview conducted by author. February 8, 2017.

Jacobsen, Rob. Interview conducted by author. November 13, 2023.

Jacobsen, Steve. Email message to author. March 1, 2024.

Jordan, Jeff. Email message to author. September 21, 2023.

Kennedy, Jan Merz. Interview conducted by author. October 6, 2023.

Kettlekamp, Tom. Participant in focus group discussion with author. November 13, 2023.

Kingdon, Harold. Email message to author. October 5, 2023.

LaDine, Jeff. Interview conducted by author. September 26, 2023.

Liddick, Dean. Interview conducted by author. October 12, 2023.

MacBeth, Wayne. Interview conducted by author. February 1, 2024.

Mahoney, Judy Tennant. Interview conducted by author. October 9, 2023.

Makin, Gregg. Email message to author. December 2023.

Manikas-Foster, Martha. Email message to author. November 2023.

Martin, Troy. Interview conducted by author. March 1, 2024.

Massey, Charles. Interview conducted by author. October 31, 2023.

Mullen, Andrew. Email messages to author. January 2024.

Mullen, James. Participant in focus group discussion with author. November 13, 2023.

Mullen, Larry. Interview conducted by author. November 1, 2023.

Mullen, Shirley. Email message to author. April 5, 2024.

Nelson, Janet Franz. Email message to author. November 28, 2016.

Nichols, Tim. Interview conducted by author. October 12, 2023.

Oehrig, Becca Thorn. Email message to author. November 2016.

Ohl, Mark. Email message to author. October 2023.

Parlett, Ray. Interview conducted by author. October 12, 2023.

Pocock, Dick. Participant in focus group discussion with author. November 13, 2023.

Roederer, Sandy. Interview conducted by author. October 14, 2023.

Roorbach, Doug. Email message to author. November 2023.

Ruth, Rob. Interview conducted by author. November 8, 2023.

Sayers, Brian. Email message to author. November 2023.

Segool, Brian. Email message to author. October 2023.

Shannon, Fred. Interview conducted by author. October 13, 2023.

Smith, Tedd. Interview conducted by author. October 6, 2023.

Spahn, Patricia. Interview conducted by author. October 10, 2023.

Stockin, Phil. Participant in focus group discussion with author. November 13, 2023.

Taylor, Ed. Interview conducted by author. October 12, 2023.

Tennies, Janet Carlson. Email message to author. December 3, 2016.

Walters, Mike. Text messages to author. February 2, 2024.

Wright, Meg Martino. Email messages to author. January 2024.

Young, Betty Bowser. Interview conducted by author. November 22, 2023.

Young, Paul. Email message to author. February 12, 2024.